The Enchanted Garden

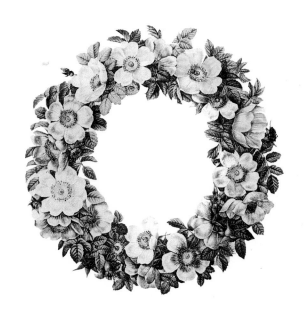

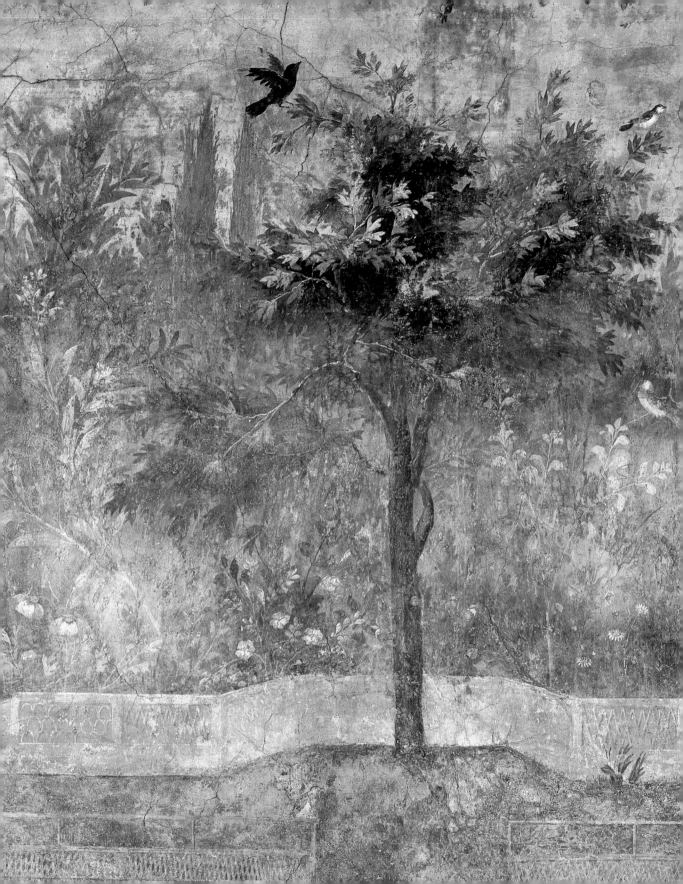

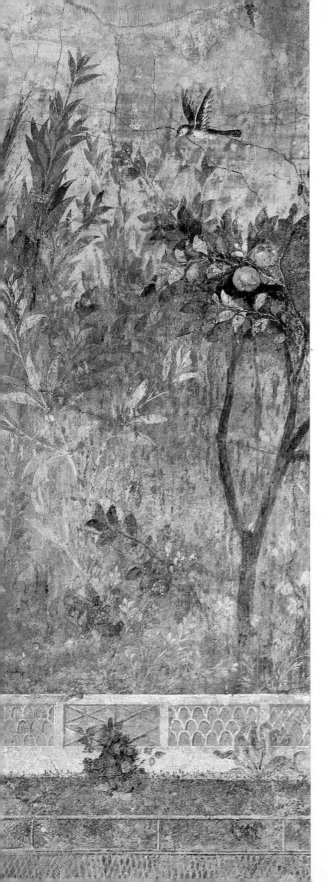

Bryan Holme

The Enchanted Garden

Images of Delight

With 94 illustrations,
43 in colour

Thames and Hudson

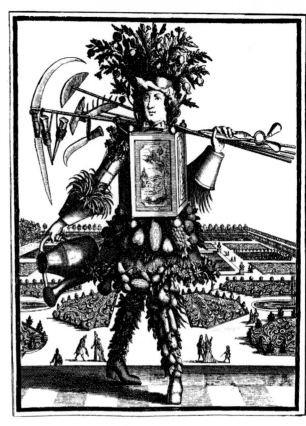

Gardener Costume. Nicolas de Larmessin. French, 17th c.

Filmset in Great Britain by August Filmsetting
Printed and bound in Italy by Imago

Frontispiece: One of the earliest and most
charming European garden scenes, this fresco
once decorated the walls of an underground room
in the summer villa of Augustus Caesar's wife,
Livia, at Prima Porta, near Rome. An oak tree
stands in the middle of the garden, and among
the other trees and flowers here (and on the other
three walls not shown) are the pomegranate,
quince, palm, oleander, pine, spruce, poppy, iris,
violet and rose. The birds are so alive we can all
but hear them singing.

Page 1. *A Rose Wreath.* From *Les Roses,* Paris 1817. Pierre-Joseph
Redouté. French, 1759–1840

Frontispiece: Roman Garden (detail). Fresco from Casa di Livia, Rome.
Second half of 1st c. BC

This is an art book for garden lovers, as well as a garden book for art lovers, young and old. With little exaggeration, it can be said that every kind of beauty, delight and fantasy has been painted in one form of garden or another since Eden, which, after Botticelli's glorious vision of Flora, is where this story begins. Birds, animals, houses, castles, legends and scenes from history, music, dancing, boating, swimming, are introduced in the natural course of events as people engage in the varied activities that the gardens of the world have afforded since the beginning of time.

Gardens were hardly ever designed just to be looked at, like beautiful scenery decorating an empty stage. In fact, in the early morning before most people are up and about, nature for her part has usually seen to it that a cast of characters is already on hand. Almost certainly birds will be heard in the trees or be seen hopping about the lawn, soon to be joined by a squirrel or a rabbit, perhaps, a butterfly or cat or dog. These and other familiar faces have a way of showing up in the garden, together or one by one – as they do in this book.

We are apt to think of the garden today in terms of a small area, possibly with room enough for raising a few vegetables and flowers – an ideal spot in which the family can play safely, enjoy picnics, entertain friends, or relax in the shade or sun. But in centuries past, the gardens of a stately home, palace, even sometimes of the so-called 'summer cottage', occupied an enormous park-like setting such as surround many of the historic houses now open to the public.

These enchanted gardens, often the dream worlds of kings, and certainly of those with princely incomes, were designed with different areas for different pastimes: acres of sweeping lawns for carefree games, running and laughter, paths for riding on horseback, grottoes to cool off in, nooks for sitting quietly in, thinking or reading, terraces for parties, dancing or gazing at the stars, pools to toss coins into for a wish to come true, and everywhere majestic trees and bright borders of flowers lining avenues or paths leading to a river, lake or pond – all this awaiting the artist to get out his canvas and paint.

Plays have been acted in gardens, ballets danced, operas sung, fêtes staged, banquets held, fireworks displayed. Fountains play in some gardens, lovers in others. The Italians invented waterworks that sent up jets higher than houses, and Louis XIV, the 'Sun King' of France, outdid every other court in Europe with his magnificent gardens at Versailles. So vast were these gardens that one lake alone was wide enough for large ships to engage in mock battles while the king sat comfortably back in his armchair watching the fun from the windows of the palace.

It takes imagination to see how a field, wilderness, forest or swampland might be transformed into a Versailles or other earthly paradise. And for most of us who are unlikely to see such a thing come to pass, even on the smallest of scales, it's exciting nonetheless – and certainly less trouble – to imagine how the garden of our dreams would look and then sit down to draw or paint it. Artists have done this kind of thing for centuries. No artist was present in

Eden, none saw the ancient Greek gods at play in the gardens of Parnassus, none witnessed a ring of fairies dancing on a midsummer night, or actually saw angels floating down a moonbeam onto a garden path; yet, as this book shows, the artist's imagination, together with his skill as a painter, has made each of these scenes appear both real and poetic.

Along with the fantasy and fun, this book aims to give a brief visual history of art and mankind as viewed, of course, from down the garden path.

First come the gardens of ancient Egypt, Greece and Rome, next the medieval castle gardens, followed by the large, formal gardens of Renaissance Italy and the even more elaborate ones of France. Our journey takes us across the far seas to China,

Japan, India and Persia, and back to the landscaped gardens of eighteenth-century England. Finally, after joining the Victorians in their gardens on either side of the Atlantic, we find ourselves in the smaller, more intimate gardens of today.

While the illustrations tell us a lot about gardens and the things that happen in them, about history and customs and how people have looked and dressed throughout the centuries, there is the added interest of studying every picture as a work of art.

We are told that imagination grows in 'the garden of the mind'. And when the mind is well cultivated, imagination can, like the painting of a masterpiece, fill our days, months and years with unending images of delight.

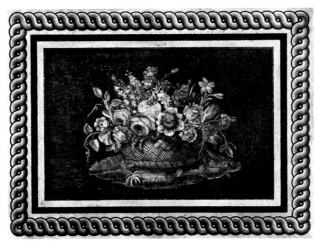

Basket of flowers. Mosaic. Roman, 2nd c. BC

A Roman mosaic showing a basket of roses, hyacinths, tulips, carnations, a double anemone and a morning glory – flowers that were evidently as popular in countries around the Mediterranean two thousand years ago as they are today.

Opposite:
'Lightly Flora walks the earth, and buds and blossoms appear wherever she passes.' This detail

from Botticelli's famous painting, *Spring*, shows Zephyrus, the West Wind, seizing the fleeing nymph, Chloris who, at his touch, is transformed into Flora – the figure standing at her side, crowned and wreathed in flowers. Even the edge of Flora's robe, blown by the wind, shapes itself into outlines of leaves and petals. The painting has been taken not only to symbolize spring (the season of the West Wind), but also the springtime of the planet earth.

Spring (detail). Sandro Botticelli.
Italian, 1444–1510

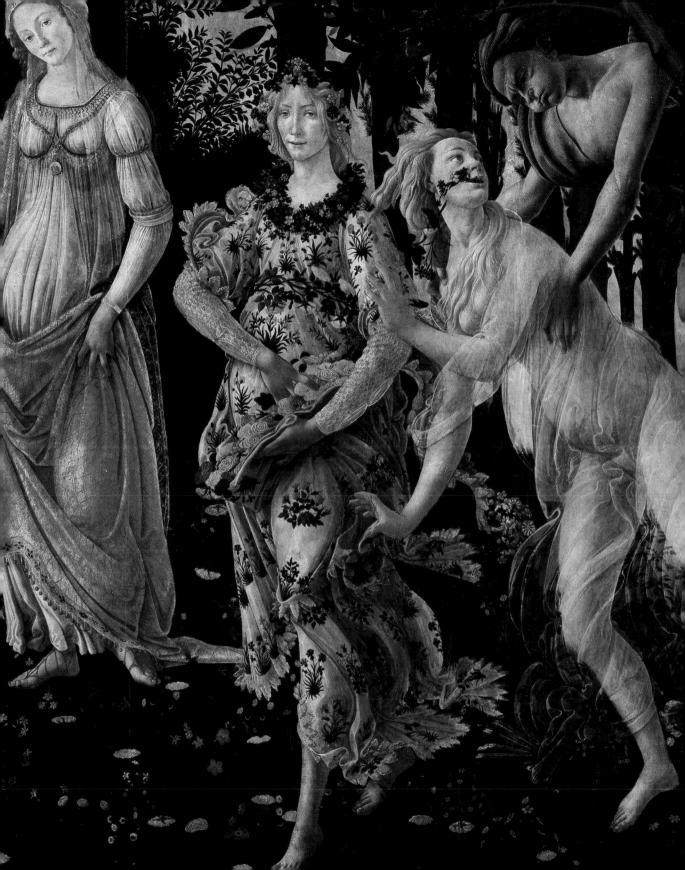

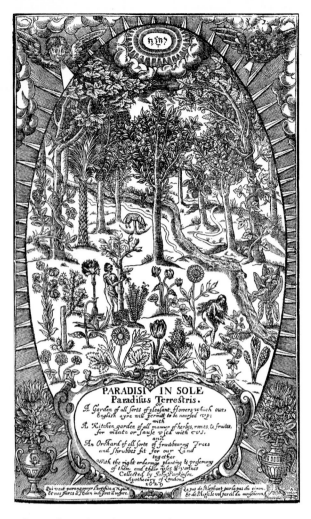

Title page from John Parkinson's *Paradisi in Sole Paradisus Terrestris*, London 1629

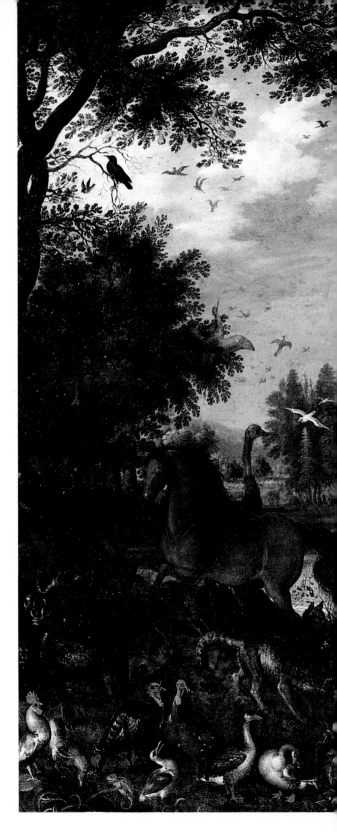

The Bible tells us that God created the first garden – in Eden. Every imaginable tree, flower, fruit and vegetable grew there. In John Parkinson's drawing made in 1629, cacti grow beside lilies, and a pineapple beside a tulip.

At right, Adam and Eve take the stage beneath the forbidden tree, there to enact the first human drama as related in Genesis. Not only are Adam and Eve at peace with the animals, but the animals themselves are at peace with one another.

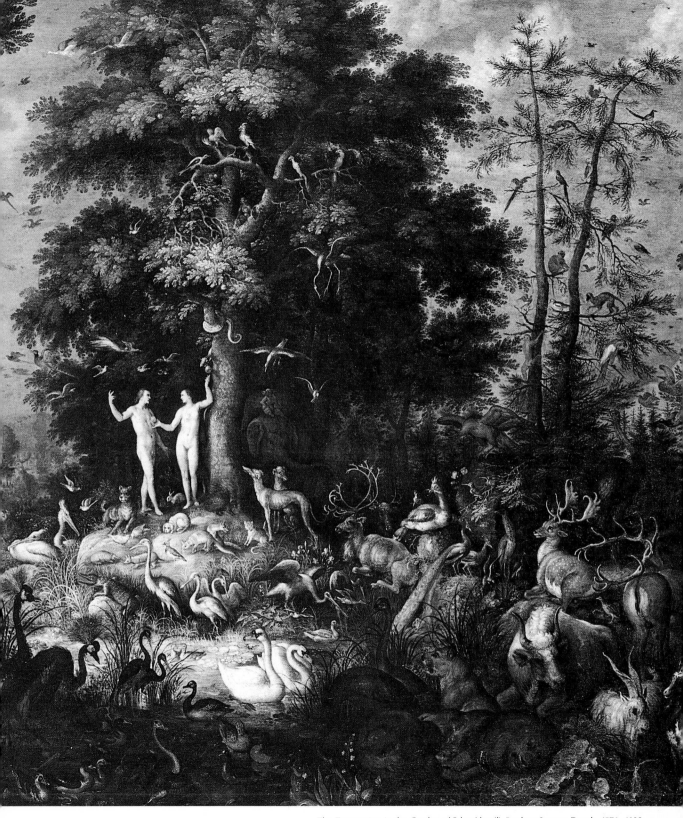

The Temptation in the Garden of Eden (detail). Roelant Savery. Dutch, 1576–1639

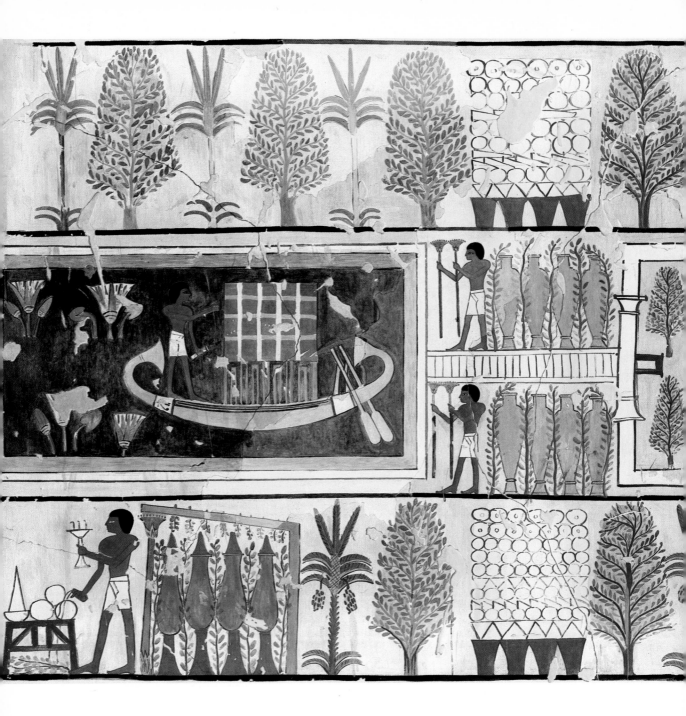

In the days of the ancient Pharaohs, this garden scene decorated the tomb of Minnakht, overseer of the granaries of Egypt. In the middle, a narrow flight of steps, bordered by tall urns, leads from the house down to the pool where a boat bearing Minnakht's coffin lies at anchor. Ceremonial bundles of papyrus reeds are carried by three of his servants.

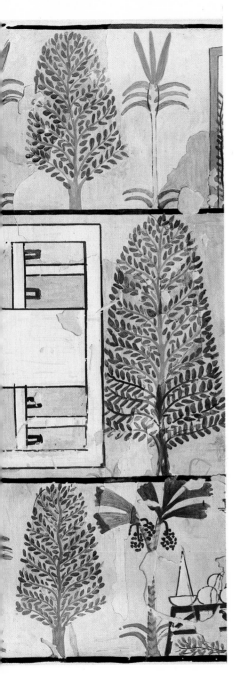

Funeral Ceremony in a Temple Garden (detail).
Copy of a mural from the Tomb of
Minnakht, Thebes. Egyptian, c. 1475 BC

At approximately the same time, across the Mediterranean in Crete, another unknown artist painted this blue bird surrounded by reeds and irises. The flower, one of the oldest known in art, was named after Iris, the Greek Goddess of the Rainbow. In Egypt the iris meant 'eloquence', and on special occasions bunches of them were used to decorate the brow of the Sphinx.

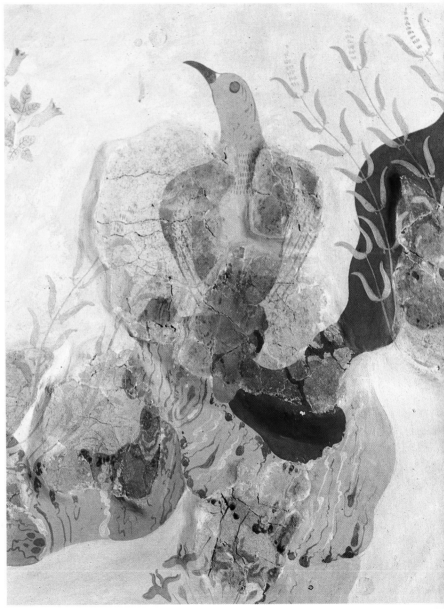

Blue Bird. Fresco from Knossos.
Cretan, c. 1500 BC

11

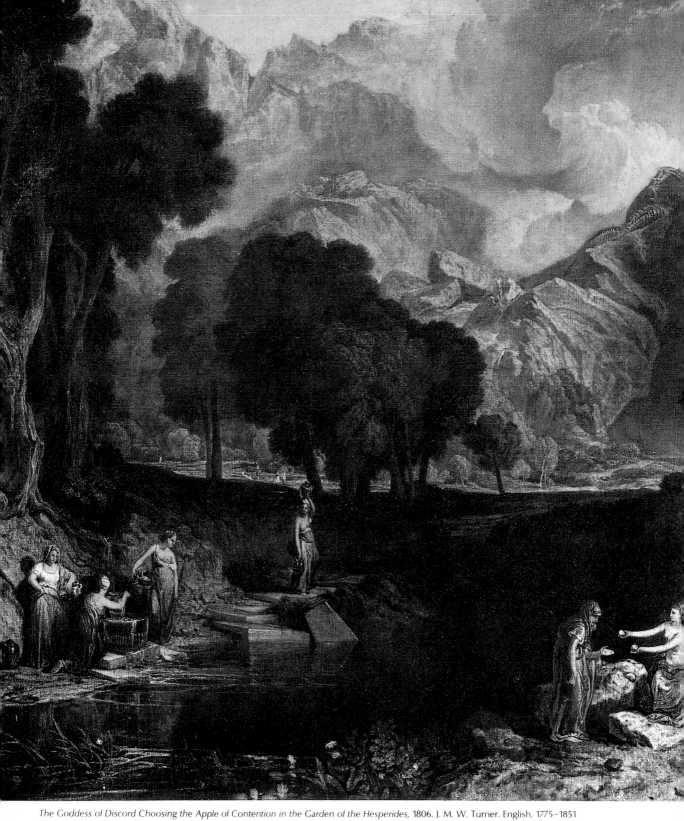

The Goddess of Discord Choosing the Apple of Contention in the Garden of the Hesperides, 1806. J. M. W. Turner. English, 1775–1851

The gardens of the gods are usually seen as open landscapes surrounded by mountains leading to the heavens. Hercules visited this one in his search for the golden apples. Here the goddess Eris is choosing the apple of contention, or strife, from one of the Hesperides.

Below, the god Apollo pursues his love, Daphne. Afraid of marriage, she cries out to her father, Peneus: 'Open the earth to enclose me, or change my form which has brought me into this danger.' A stiffness at once seizes her limbs, bark encloses her bosom, her hair turns to leaves, her arms to branches. A heartbroken Apollo swears: 'Since you cannot be my wife, you shall assuredly be my tree. I will wear you for my crown . . . and will decorate with you my harp and quiver.'

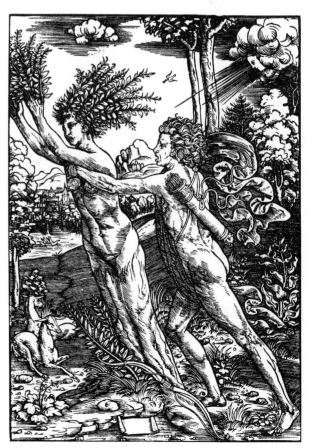

Apollo and Daphne. Woodcut. Jacopo Ripanda. Italian, 16th c.

13

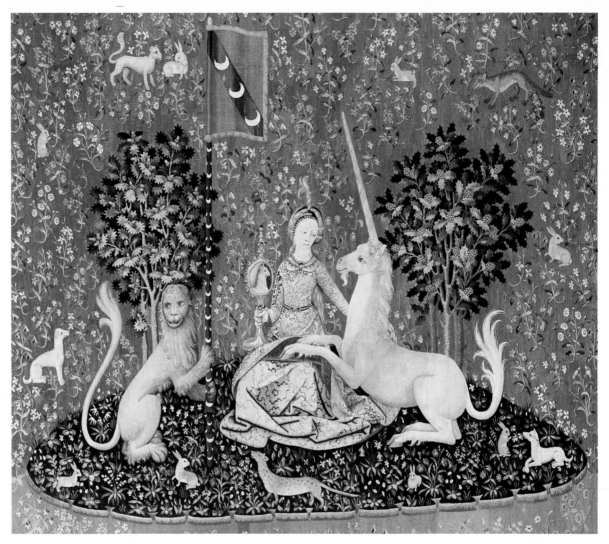

Lady and the Unicorn: the Sense of Sight. Tapestry (detail). French, late 15th c.

With the passing of the Greek and Roman civilizations, it is sometimes said that art went to sleep for a thousand years, to be awakened by the Church in the twelfth century with the building of the Gothic cathedrals, and by Italy in the fourteenth and fifteenth centuries when a renewed interest in literature and art produced such glorious masterpieces as Botticelli's *Spring* on page 7.

The spirit of this Renaissance, or rebirth, soon spread to northern Europe, where these two

tapestries were woven. The lady seated 'in a flowery mead', above, holds a mirror in which the unicorn's face is reflected. In Christian symbolism, the lion sometimes represented Christ, and the unicorn the Virgin Mary.

The lady at right, holding a falcon on her wrist, looks every inch a fairytale princess – elegantly dressed in a gown trimmed with ermine and wearing 'a jewelled tower of magnificence' on her pretty head.

Lady with a Falcon. Tapestry (detail). Franco-Flemish, c. 1420–35

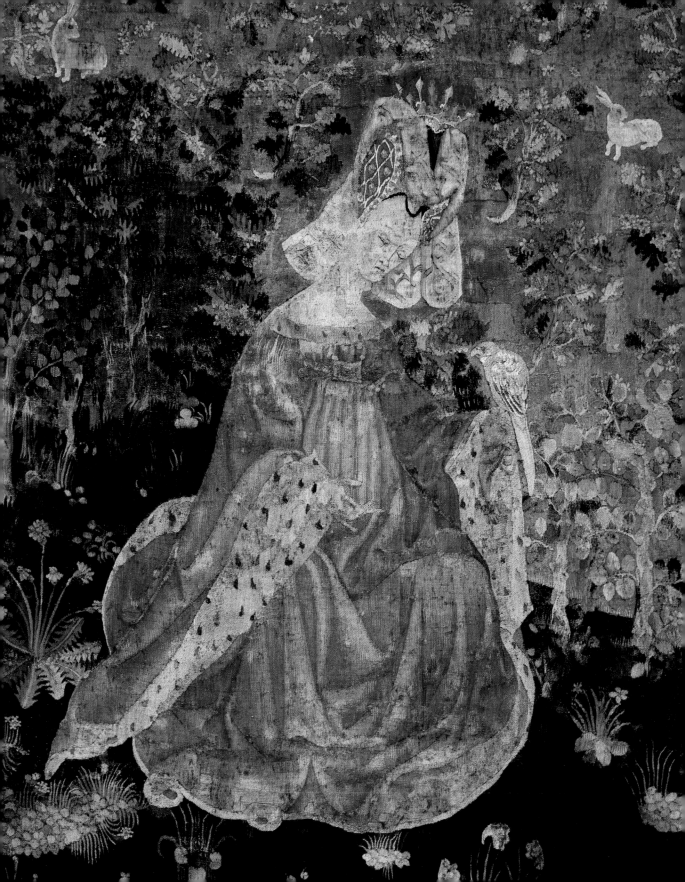

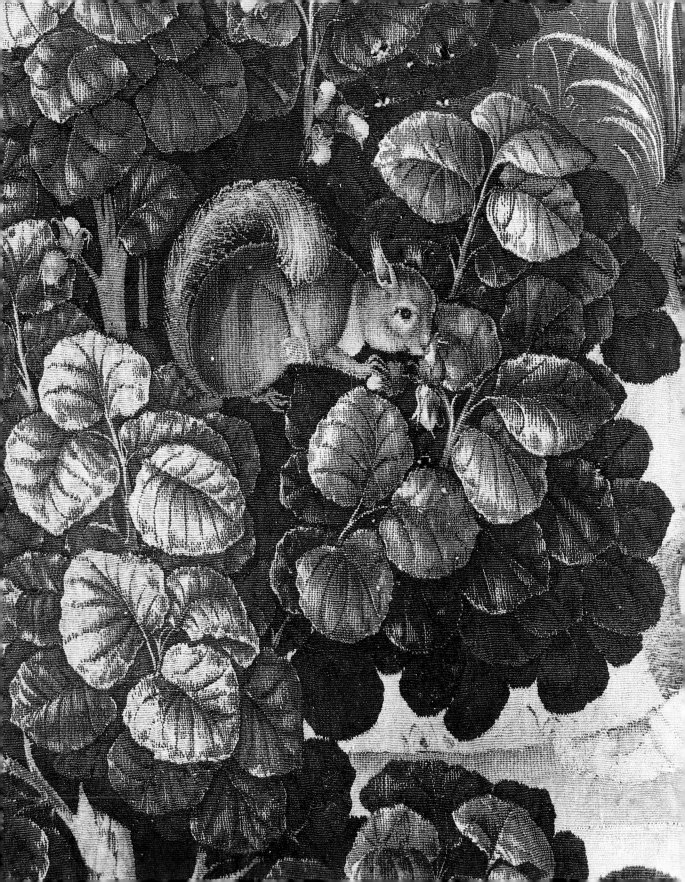

March. Miniature.
Simon Bening of Bruges.
Flemish, c. 1530

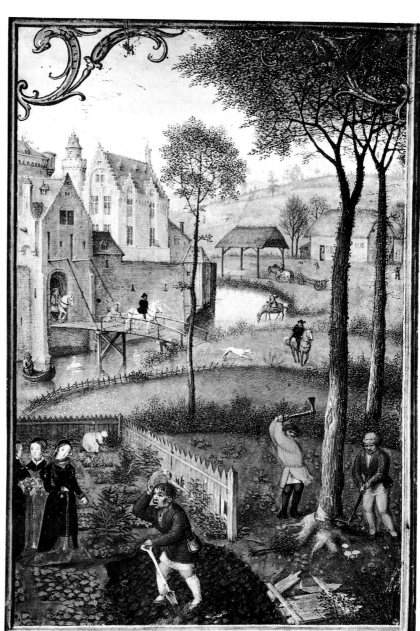

The detail, at left, from another famous tapestry, shows a squirrel up a nut tree which could well have grown in the medieval castle grounds at right. There two men are felling a tree, not merely to get wood for the fireplace, but also to give the new plot being dug by the gardener enough sunlight for plants to grow. The scene, representing the month of March, is one of twelve miniatures painted around 1530 for a calendar in an illustrated prayer book.

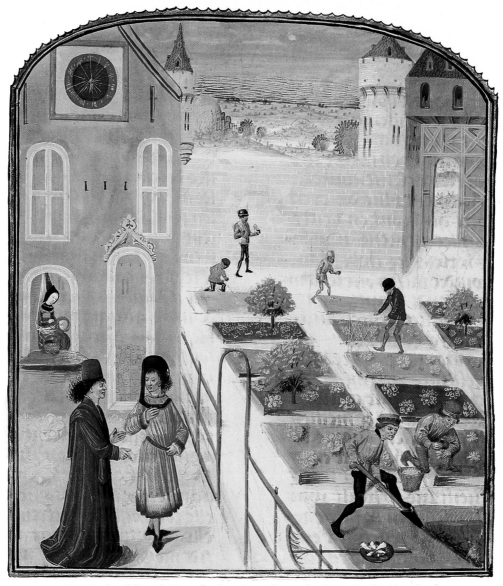

Castle Garden. Philippe de Mazerolles. From Petrus Crescentius, *De Rustica.* Flemish, 15th c.

Another castle garden bustling with activity as beds are made ready and vegetables, herbs and fruit trees are planted. The illustration is from 'The Book of Rural Profits', written in the fifteenth century by Petrus Crescentius, the gentleman we see at left chatting with the owner of the castle whose wife, wearing the stylish hennin headdress of the day, sits sewing at the open window.

Back across another garden, through a window of the same period as the castle above, the portrait at right offers a charming close-up view of a young Florentine couple who, if it weren't for the clothes, look exactly as a similar couple would today.

Man and Woman at a Casement, early 1440s.
Filippo Lippi. Italian, c. 1406–69

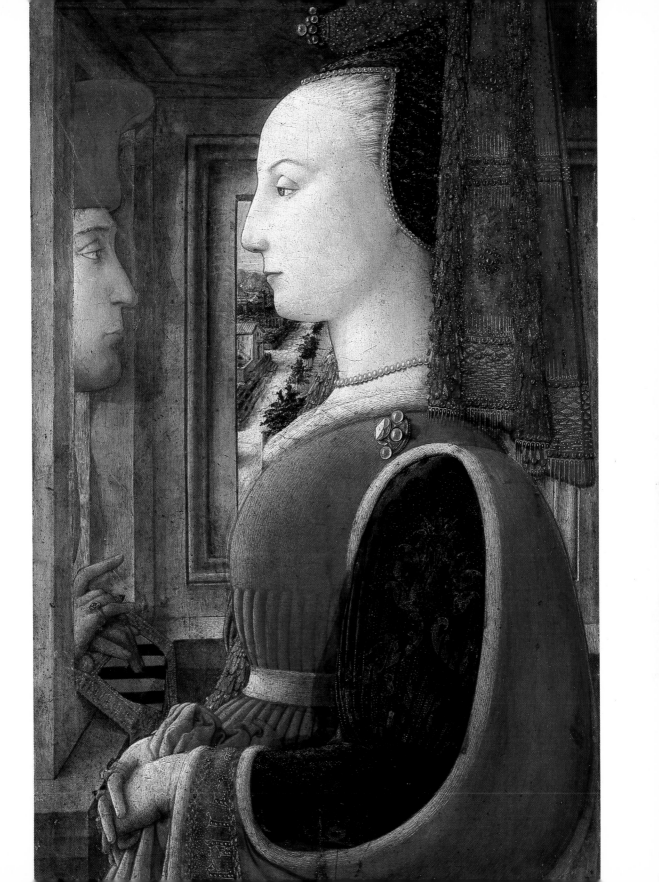

Two lovers are about to hold hands as the dog sits faithfully at his master's feet. Typical of the medieval garden are the small Gothic fountain, the urn holding carnations, and the clipped evergreen in the background. The artist made much of the lady's dress, arranging the ample folds in a design that suggests a maze, with its intricate network of paths bordered by tall hedges, specially designed for people to get lost in – and to have the fun of going round and round in circles, while puzzling their way out of it. On page 34 a real maze fills a whole island in the middle of a river.

The medieval walled garden, at right, is the setting for an allegory, or story told in symbols. It comes from a manuscript entitled 'Love's Game of Chess', originally created for King Francis I of France. The youth has been led by his teacher to the Garden of Nature, at the entrance to which stands Nature herself, holding the key. Once inside the garden, the student must decide which kind of life he will follow: the life represented by Venus, Goddess of Love (standing naked under the tree), by Pallas, Goddess of Wisdom (seated), or by Juno (left) who as queen of the gods is Virtue itself.

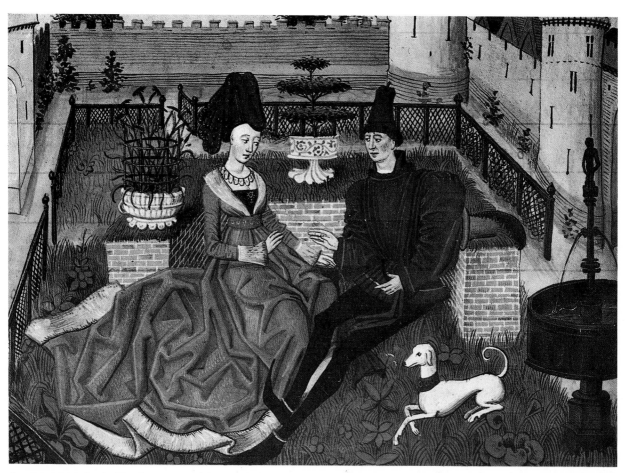

Couple in a Castle Garden (detail). From *Renaud de Montalban*. Miniature. French, 15th c.

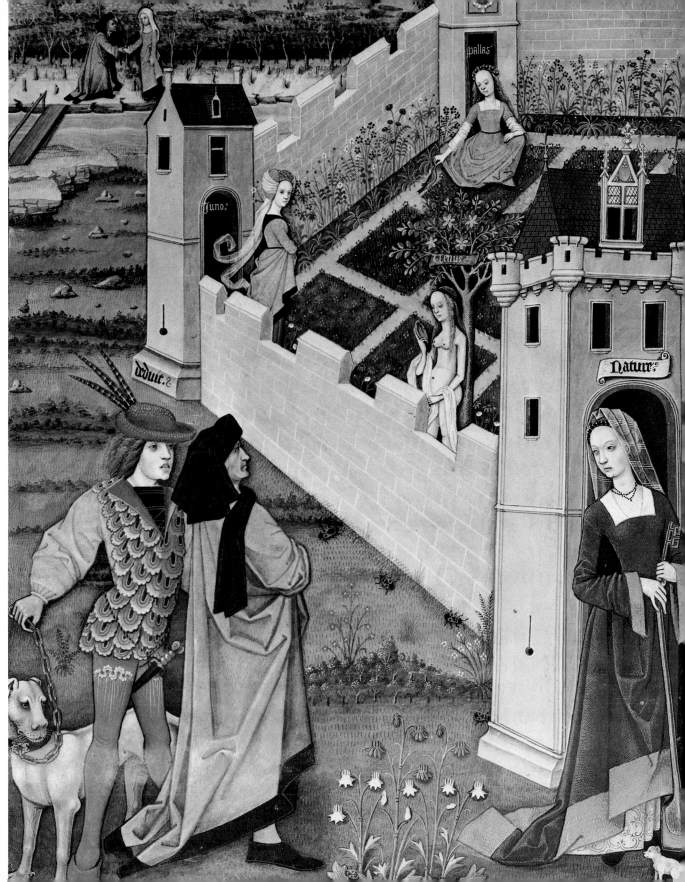

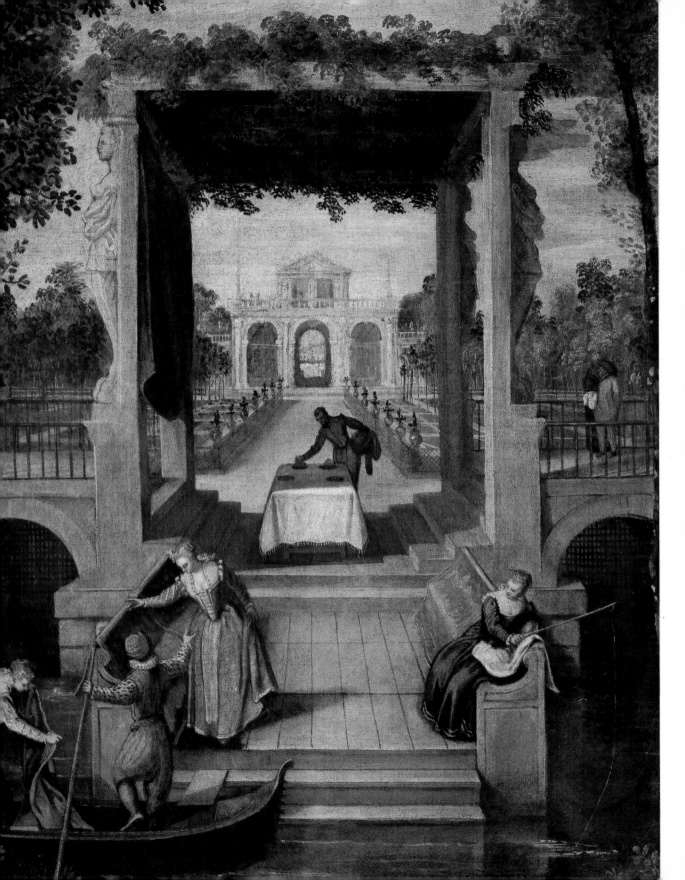

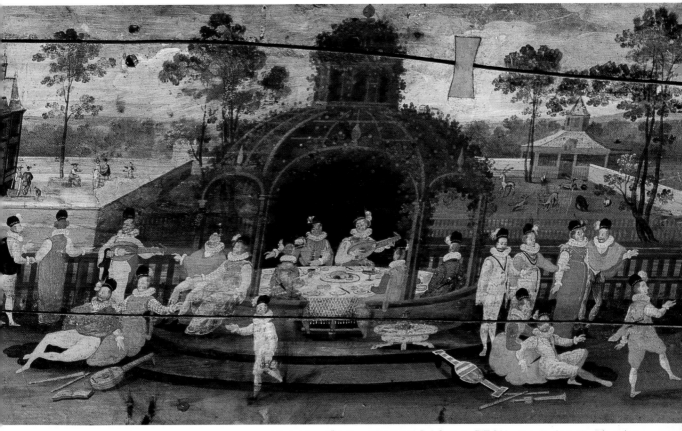

Musical Party (detail), c. 1586. Painting on a virginal made by Hans Ruckers. Flemish, 16th c.

The sixteenth century saw the development of the pleasure garden; the larger and more formal it became, the more elaborate the meals and entertainments held there. After dining in the loggia, or arcade, of the sunny Venetian garden at left, one lady tries her luck with a fishing line while another descends the steps to take a cooling ride in a gondola.

Garden Scene. Attributed to Benedetto Caliari. Italian, 16th c.

A medieval garden feast is in progress above, with entertainment by musicians with lutes, flutes and shawms – the double-reeded instruments shown at bottom right. The painting decorates the inside lid of a double virginal, or small harpsichord, made in 1581.

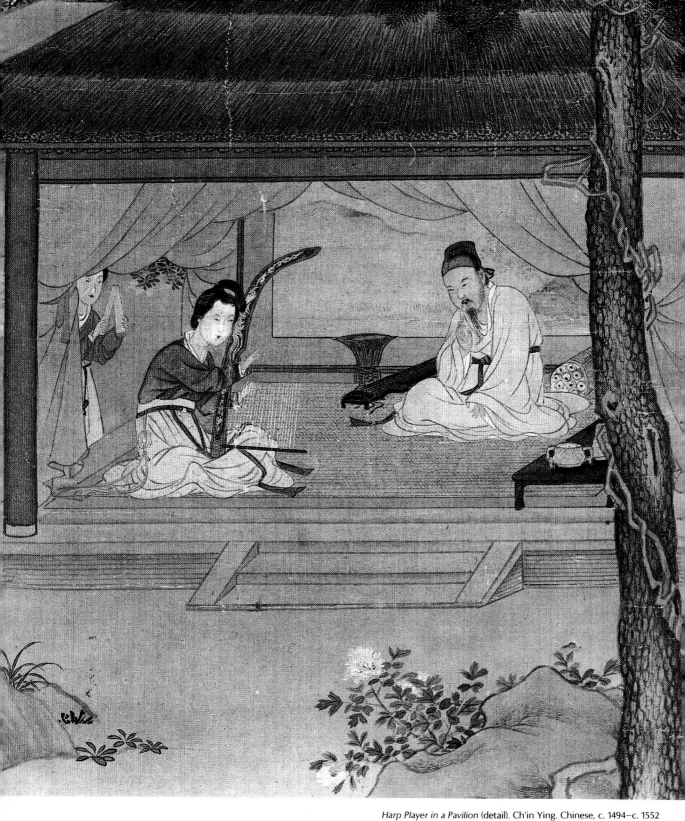

Harp Player in a Pavilion (detail). Ch'in Ying. Chinese, c. 1494–c. 1552

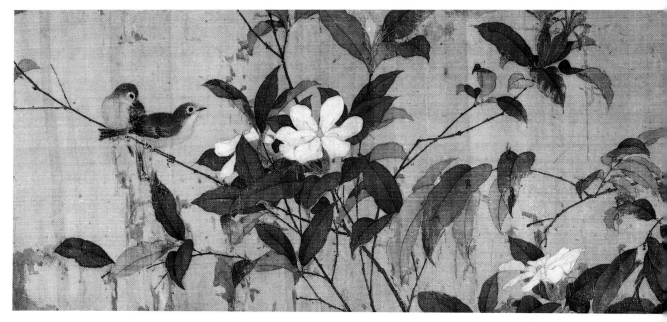

Gardenia and Birds (detail). Attributed to the Emperor Hui Tsung (reigned AD 1101–26). Chinese

And at left we see how very different a garden with musical entertainment looked on the other side of the world – in China. Despite the modern-looking architecture – with those simple lines the Chinese and Japanese have always used – the painting is of approximately the same period as the European scene on the previous page. The harpist is looking towards the peony bush, and perhaps it's from the flowers that she is drawing inspiration to play?

The study of two birds and a gardenia, above, is so simple, natural and timeless that it could have been painted hundreds of years ago, or just yesterday. In fact, it belongs to the twelfth century and is attributed to Hui Tsung who, like many Chinese Emperors, was a skilled artist as well as ruler of his country.

A dog might turn up with a feather in its mouth almost anywhere, but the soft and delicate, yet clear brushwork tells us at once that if the puppy, below, wasn't painted in China, then it must either have been in Japan or (as is the case) Korea.

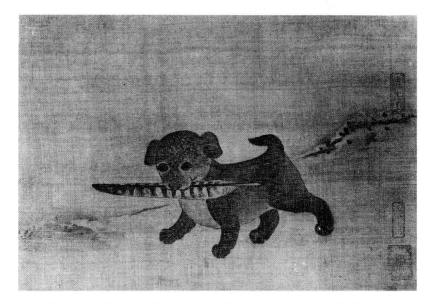

Puppy Playing with a Pheasant Feather. Hanging scroll, watercolour and ink on silk. Yi Om. Korean, 16th c.

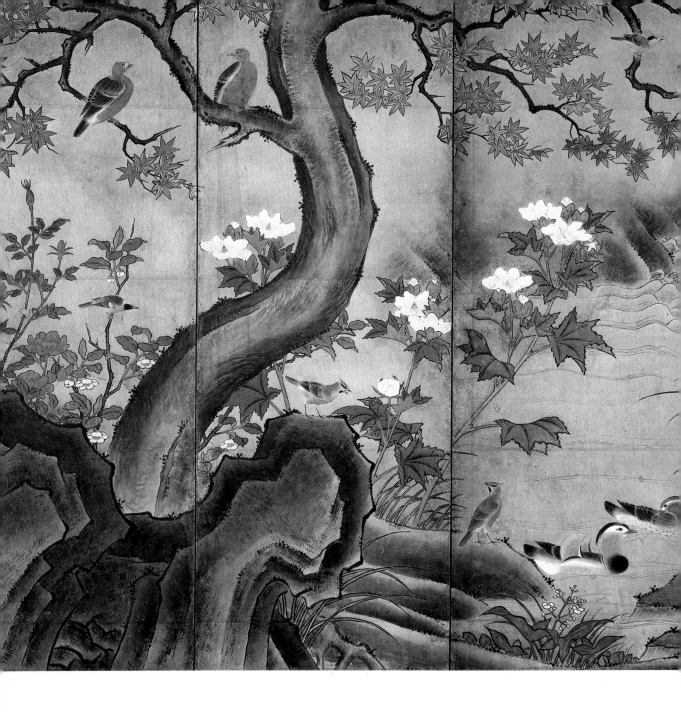

This lovely pattern of a tree at the end of a garden represents Japanese screen painting at its best. Before painting the screen itself, the artist took the most perfect specimens he could find, drew them individually, then positioned each flower, leaf and bird where it looked the most effective. To keep

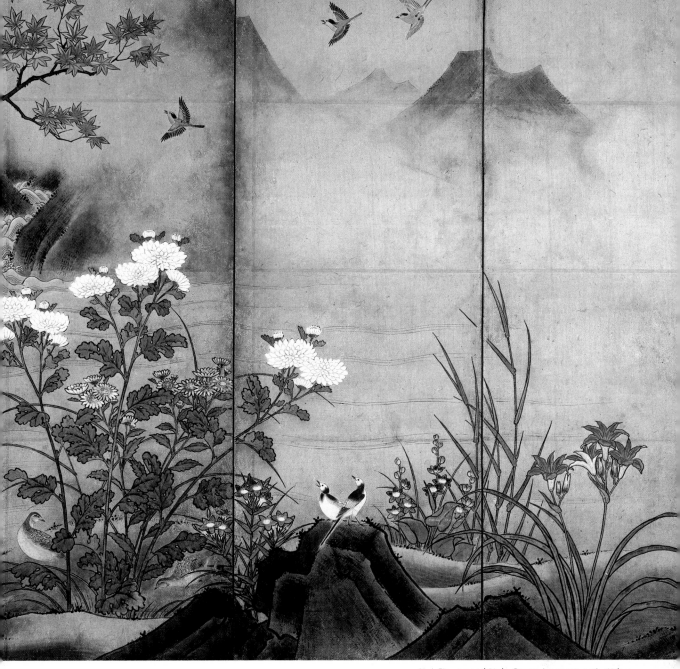

Flowers and Birds. Genga. Japanese, early 16th c.

our attention in the foreground, he merely
suggested the outline of the distant mountains and
waterfall.

It's sometimes forgotten that swimming pools are not a modern invention. The ancient Egyptians, Greeks and Romans enjoyed their swims – and so did the Persians, as this bird's-eye view of five nymphs splashing and tugging at each other clearly shows. While they enjoy themselves, others watch, play music and dance. The Persians loved bright tiles and flowers and created carpets to match, so that when winter came, they could, so to speak, pull the garden indoors with them.

In the sixteenth-century Persian garden at right, cleverly suggested by a few lightly sketched leaves and flowers, the young man, pulling gently at the corner of the lady's mantle, seems to be bidding her stay for a loving cup.

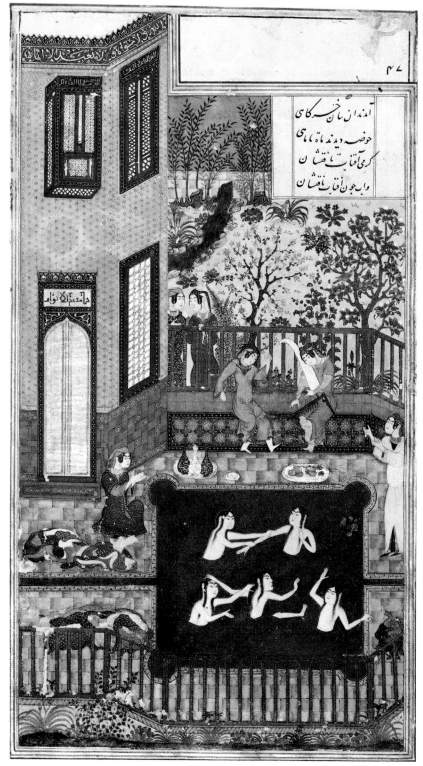

Nymphs Bathing in a Garden Pool. School of Herat, *c.* 1426. Miniature from the manuscript of Haft Paikar by Nizami. Persian

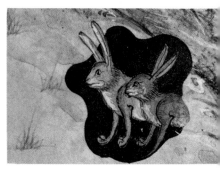

Two Rabbits. From *Kay Khosrow Rides Bihzad for the First Time.* Miniature from a *Shah-Nameh* of Ferdowsi (detail). Persian, 1525–30

Two Persian rabbits emerge from their warren to see what's what.

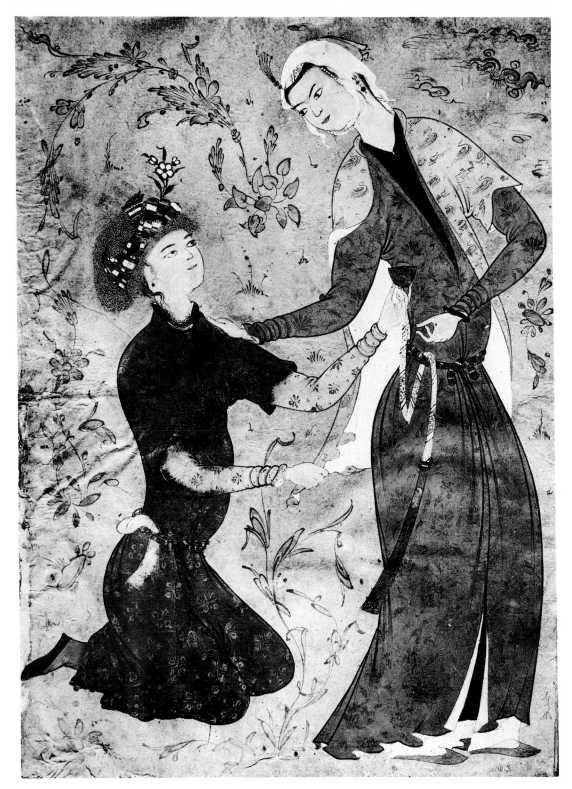

Love Scene. Ustad Muhammadi. Persian, c. 1550–75

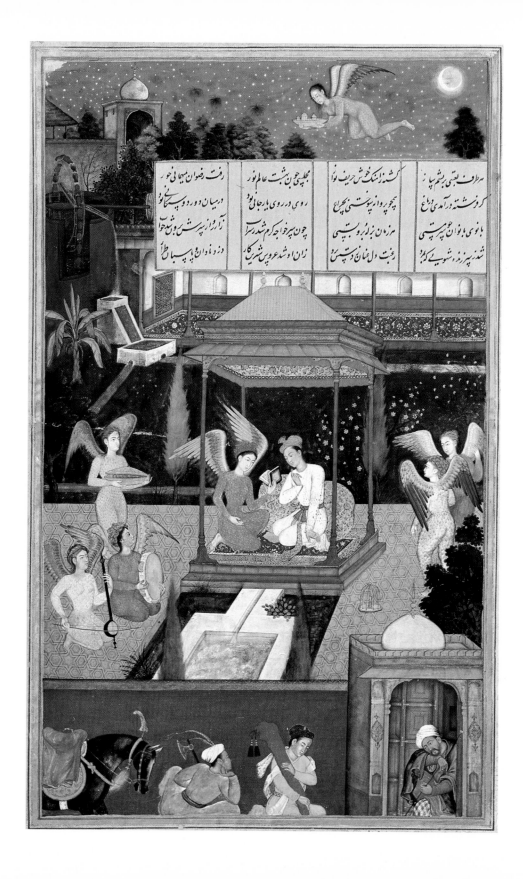

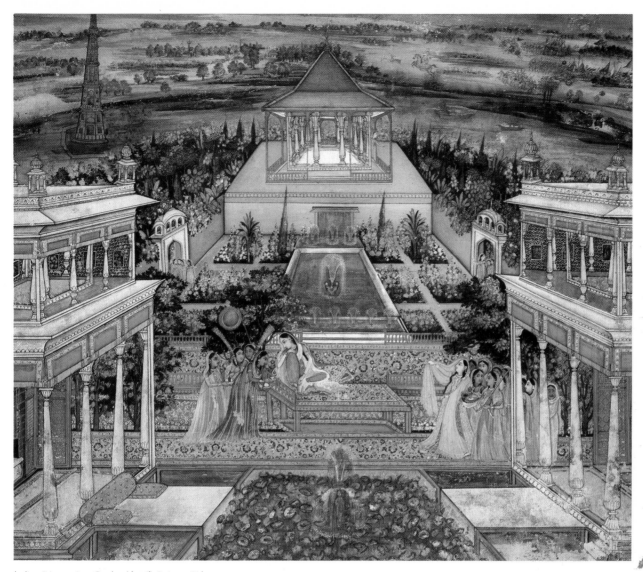

Indian Princess in a Garden (detail). Rajput, 18th c.

Under a starry sky and to the accompaniment of angelic music, King Bahram Gur visits a Persian princess in the garden of her purple palace, at left. It is easy to imagine the sound of rippling water and to smell the sweet scent of flowers filling the balmy night-time air. This exquisite miniature is a sixteenth-century Indian artist's interpretation of a scene from a classic Persian poem by Dihlavi, written two centuries earlier.

Bahram Gur Visits a Princess in the Purple Palace in the Sixth Paradise. Miniature from the *Khamseh* of Amir Khosrow Dihlavi. Indian, 1595–1600

The Indian princess above, surrounded by attendants, is receiving visitors in another garden of fairytale perfection. Masses of flowers fill the neat weedless beds, blossoming trees and shrubs reach high above the pink walls, fountains send up fan-shaped sprays to cool the air, and wherever there are no flowers, trees or glimpses of water to enjoy, jewel-like tiles and elegant pavilions dazzle the eye and imagination.

The story of the pleasure garden is also the story of flowers. So many varieties, long taken for granted in the western garden, were first discovered in eastern countries such as China, Persia and India where the gardens in the last few pages were painted. In seventeenth-century Europe, nowhere, it seems, were flowers more appreciated than in Holland, a country famous for bulb culture and its school of flower painting. The father of this school was Jan Bruegel, who painted the trees and flowers in the picture at right; the rest was done by Pieter van Avont.

The study of an iris with butterflies and grasshoppers, below, is by Jacques Le Moyne, who spent a perilous year in 1564 painting scenes in Florida, where he narrowly escaped being massacred by the Indians.

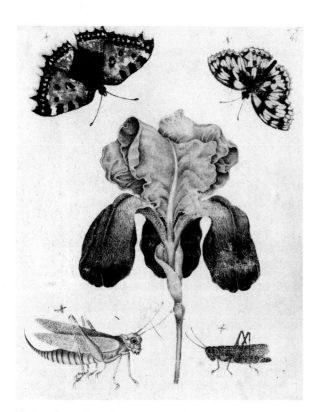

Iris, Butterflies and Grasshoppers. From a sketchbook of nature studies. Jacques Le Moyne de Morques. French, c. 1535–88

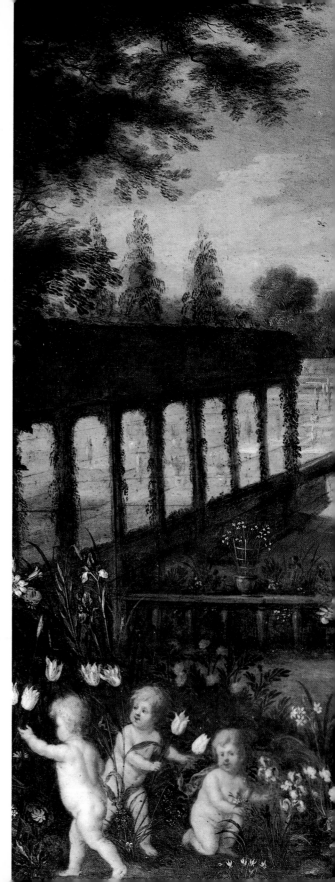

32   *Flora in a Garden* (detail).
Pieter von Avont. Flemish, 1600–52

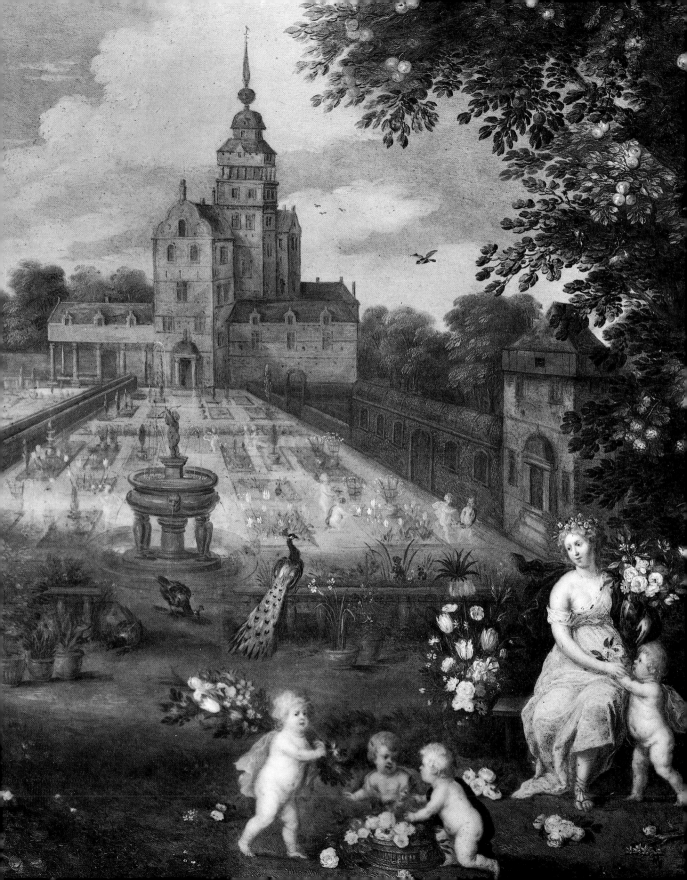

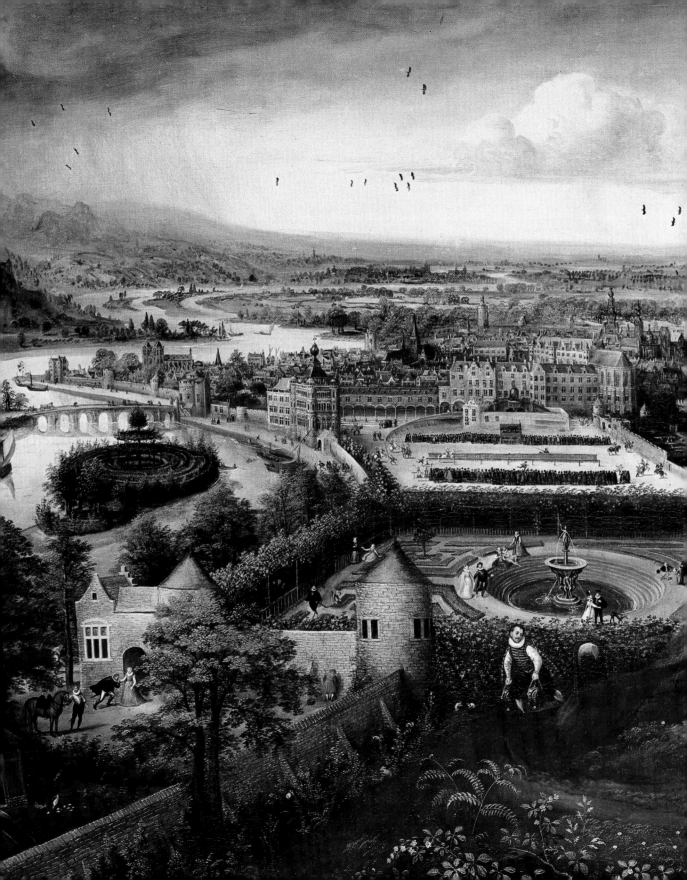

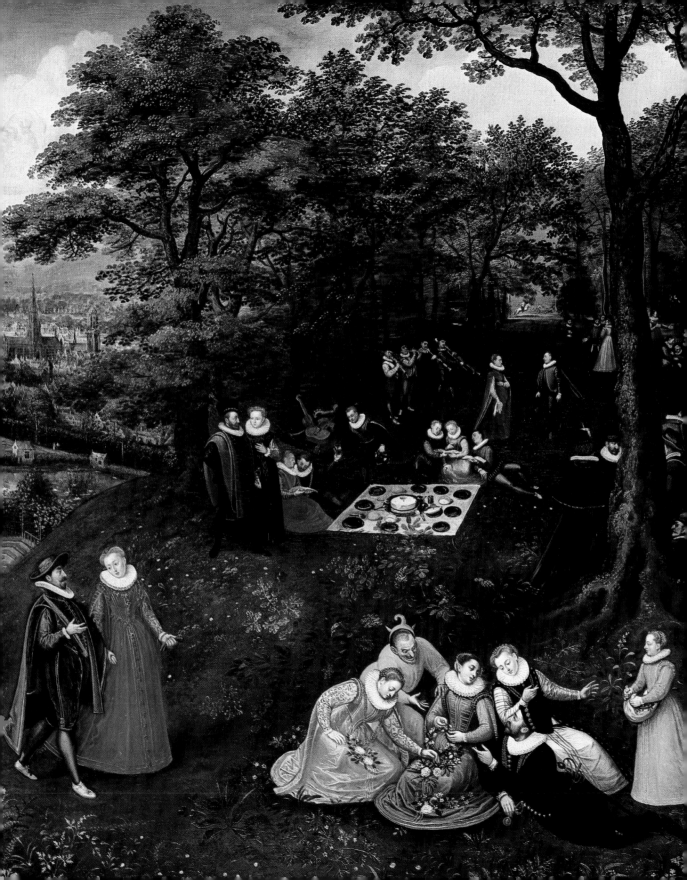

On the previous page: Many of the delights of a late medieval garden appear in the *Spring Picnic with Elegant Company*. Among these delights are: the formal garden and terraces, the square for riding and jousting, the maze (occupying a whole island), the fountain and the path leading up to the meadow, where the ladies are making daisy chains.

Spring Picnic with Elegant Company. Lucas van Valckenborch. Flemish, c. 1535–97

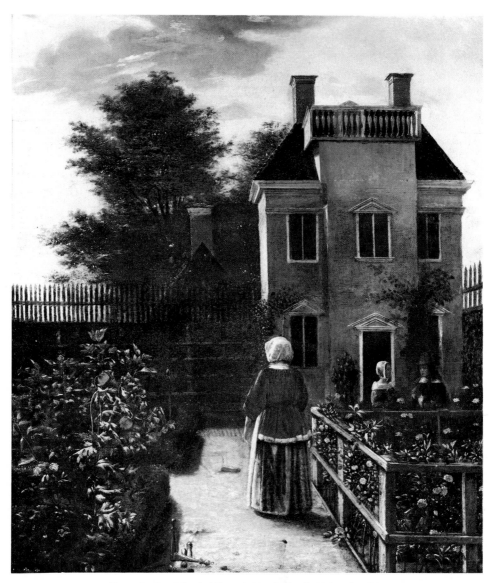

Flower Garden. School of Pieter de Hooch. Dutch, 1629 – after 1684

In contrast is the small informal seventeenth-century Dutch garden above, designed mostly for the raising and enjoyment of flowers.

At right, the lady's interest just at this moment lies neither in flowers nor skittles, but in the gentleman who has won her smile.

Game of Skittles. Pieter de Hooch. Dutch, 1629 – after 1684

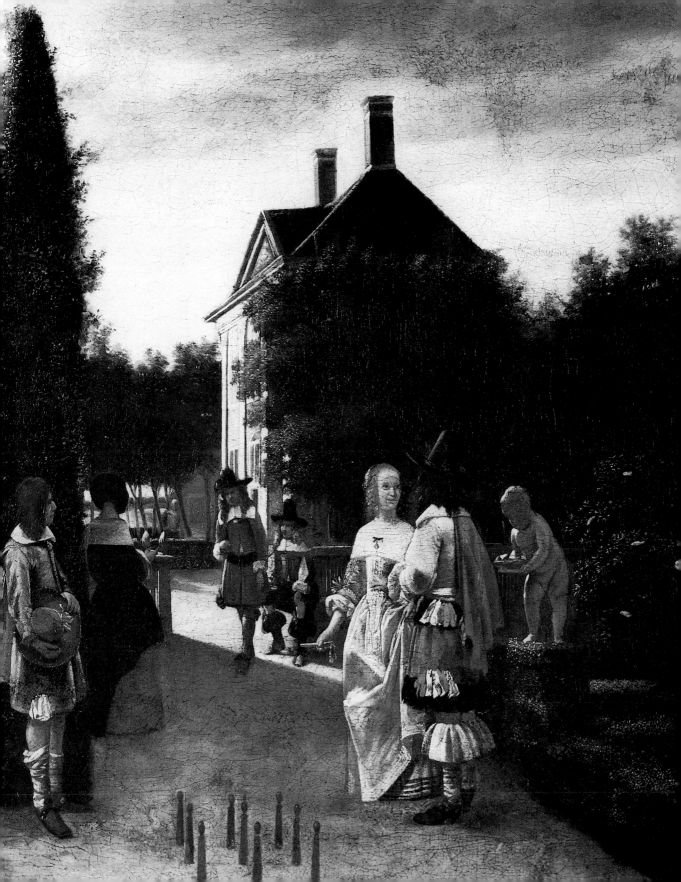

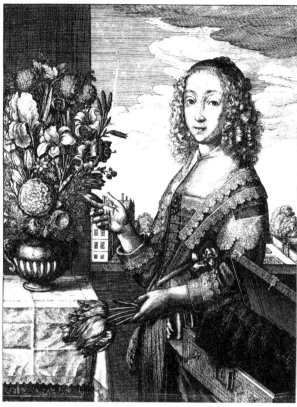

Spring, 1641. From a set of engravings showing the four seasons. Wenceslaus Hollar. Czech, 1607–77

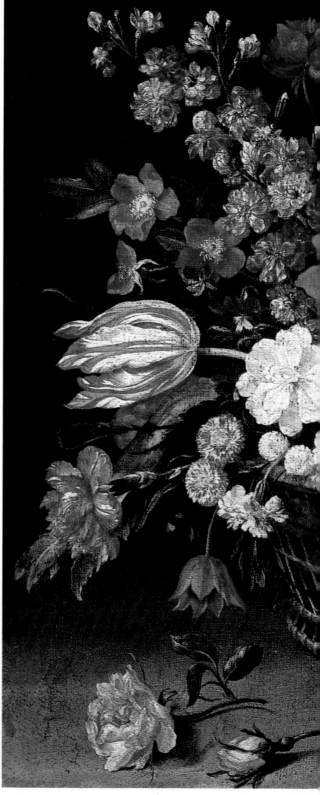

In the seventeenth century, with cultivated flowers so plentiful, it was natural for the ladies, taking their cue from the flower painters, to develop the art of indoor floral display. The lady above is putting the finishing touches to a massed arrangement in England in 1641.

At right, the French artist, Jacques Linard, although influenced by the Dutch painters, composed this arrangement of flowers in a much freer style. Seldom before had flowers formed the entire subject of a painting, but from now on bouquets and fruit became increasingly popular in their own right.

Basket of Flowers, c. 1627. Jacques Linard. French, *c.* 1600–45

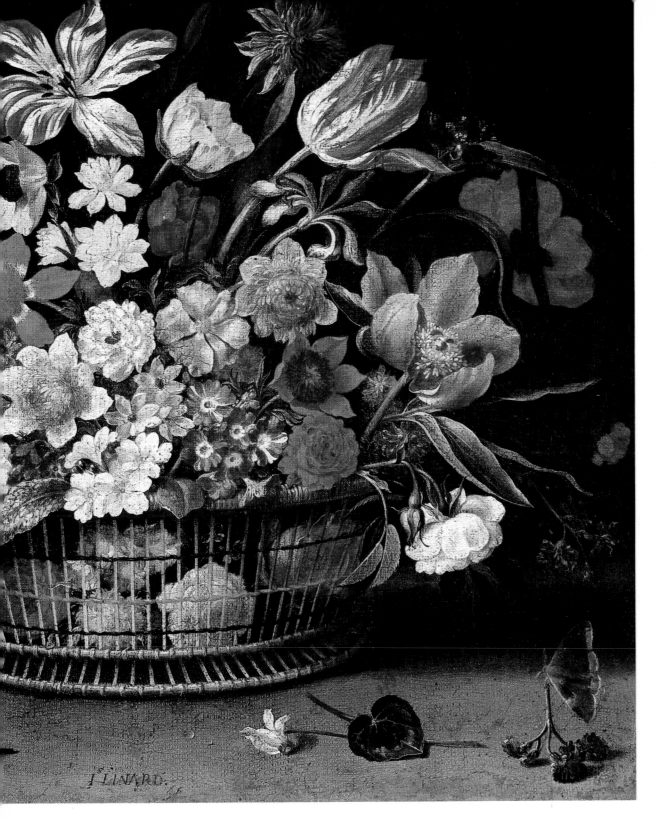

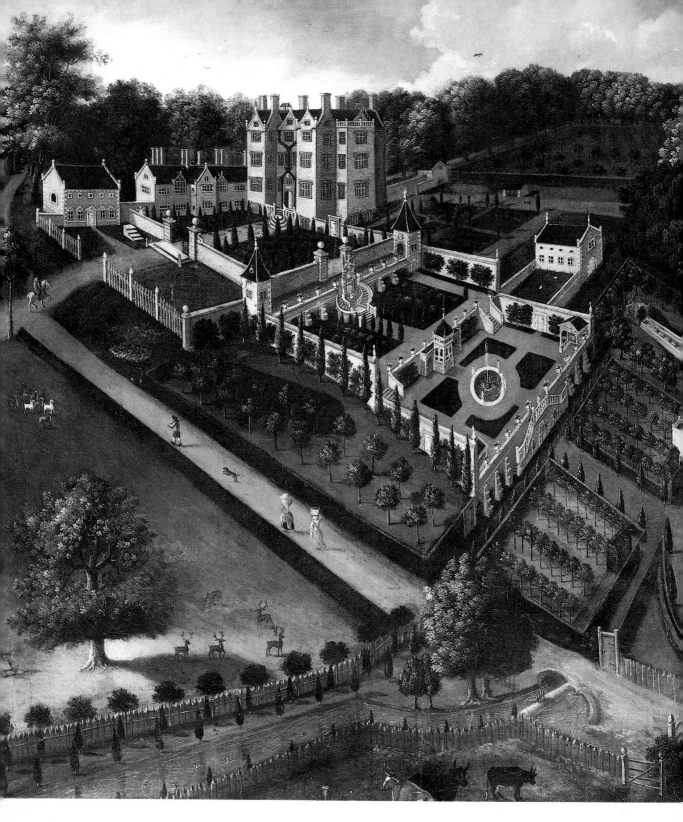

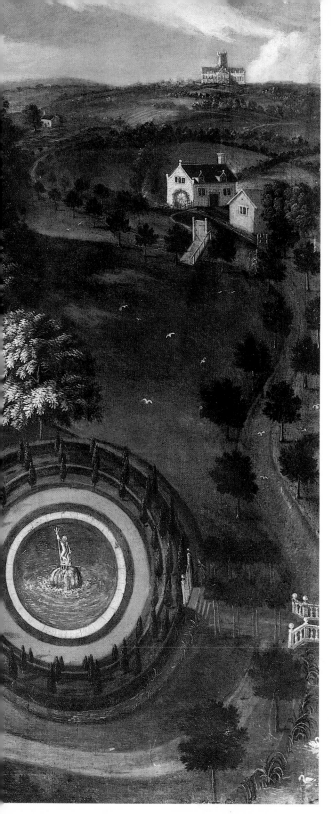

It was the fashion in seventeenth-century England for a formal Jacobean manor to feature a three-tiered garden enclosed by high brick walls. Here, in the two lower areas, are a curved baroque staircase, gazebos, bowers, and, on the walls, evenly spaced urns to hold flowers. The circular water garden at bottom right has a statue of Neptune, the Water God, for its fountain. Neatly kept orchards surround the garden.

The borderline between a pleasure garden and an orchard is a thin one, for there's as much beauty in fruit as there is in flowers. To add life to this still-life, the artist placed a spider at left and perched a blue bird above the grapes.

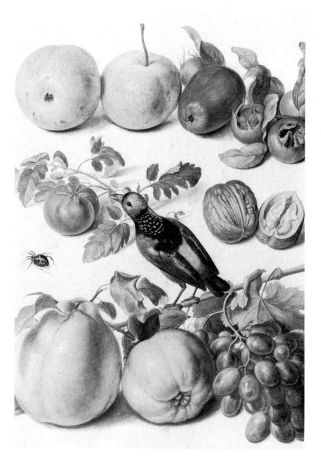

A View of Llanerch, Denbighshire, 1662. British school, 17th c.

Blue Bird with Fruit, c. 1650. Johann Walther. German, c. 1600–79

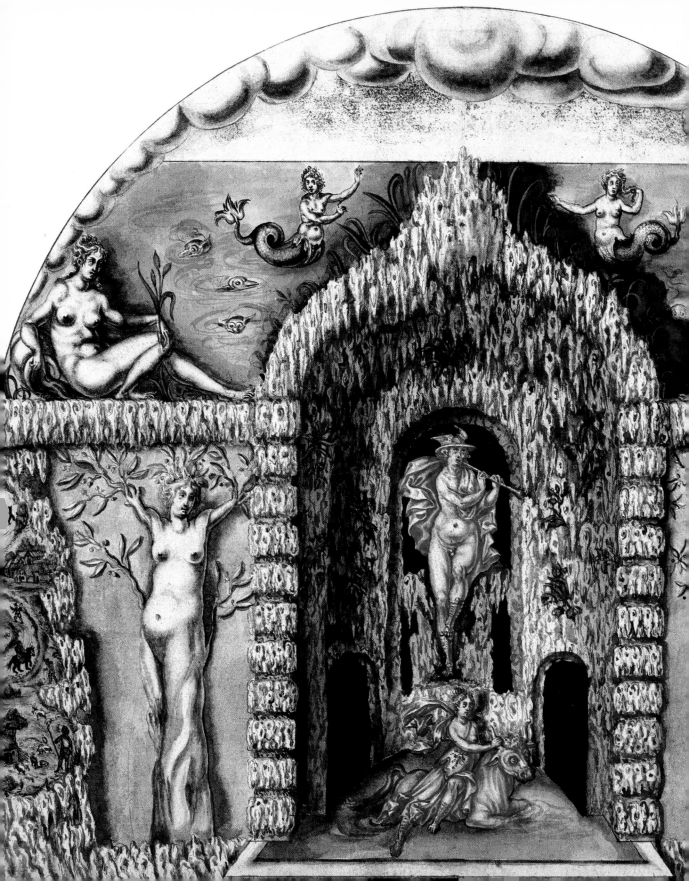

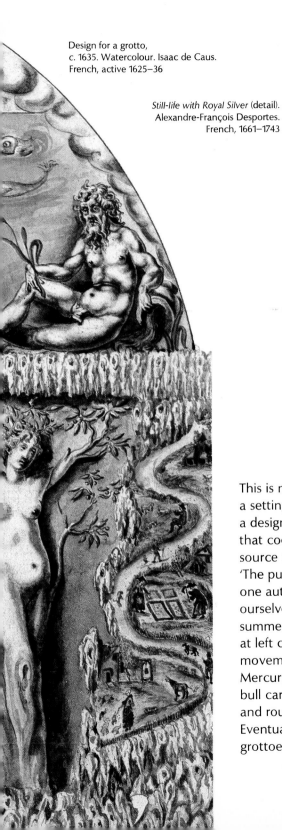

Design for a grotto,
c. 1635. Watercolour. Isaac de Caus.
French, active 1625–36

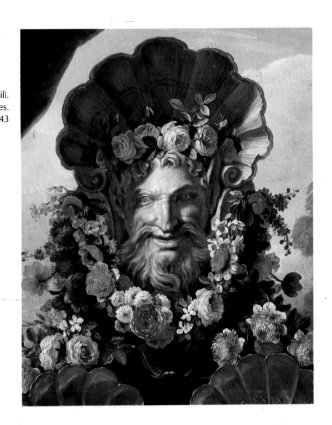

Still-life with Royal Silver (detail).
Alexandre-François Desportes.
French, 1661–1743

This is not, as one might expect, a setting for a modern ballet, but a design made in the 1630s for that cool, watery, cave-like source of delight, the grotto. 'The purpose of the grotto', said one authority, was 'to repose ourselves in the time of our summer faint heats.' If the scene at left came to life, the movement of water would make Mercury's pipe sound and the bull carry a giddy Europa round and round through the arches. Eventually the fashion for grottoes died, and in 1778 Lord Lyttelton, taking a long look down his nose at statues in a grotto, complained: 'Our climate is not fitted for the deities of Italy and Greece . . . and in a hard winter I feel for the shuddering divinities.'

The puckish face above, framed by a large shell and wreathed in flowers and smiles, might well have ornamented a grotto, but in fact appears in an oil painting *Still-life with Royal Silver* by A.-F. Desportes.

43

The most exciting man-made spectacle in the garden is the fountain. By the sixteenth century, the Italians had already invented waterworks capable of sending 'cascades from rocky heights into sculptured basins'; they had found ways to make streams of water play musical instruments (as on page 42); they also knew how to channel water through animal-shaped figures so that the creatures appeared alive; drinking, bouncing and swimming about. Mischievously too, the Italians devised systems of hidden jets that at the press of a button, or even automatically, would spurt water at the unsuspecting passer-by, wetting his clothes or catching him in the face, back or legs.

The many fountains at Versailles, the enormous park and gardens that André Le Nôtre, 'Gardener of Kings' and 'King of Gardeners', had designed for Louis XIV of France in 1662 also had their origin in Italian ingenuity.

Here is the view Louis the 'Sun King' enjoyed from his apartment in the palace. In the middle of the fountain, Apollo is seen rising above the cascading waters in a chariot drawn by four horses, and behind the octagonal pool is the vast artificial lake on which mock battles were staged for the king's amusement.

With Versailles, the art of the formal garden, fostered by the Italians, reached its peak. The

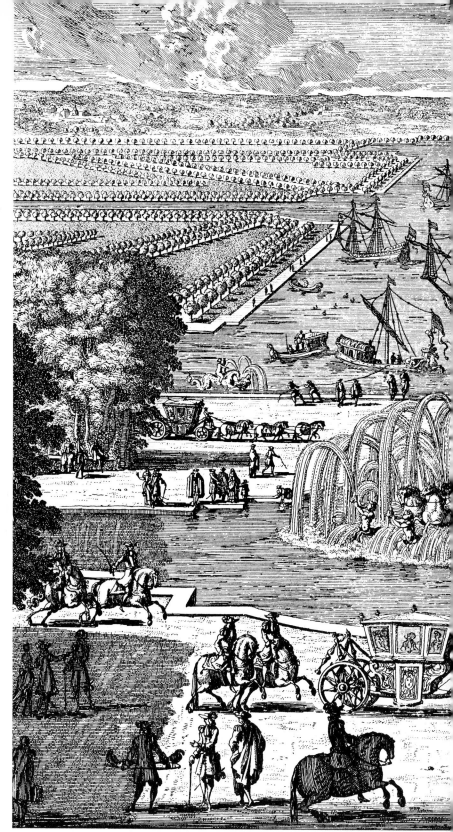

The Apollo Pool (detail). Engraving. Pérelle. French, 17th c.

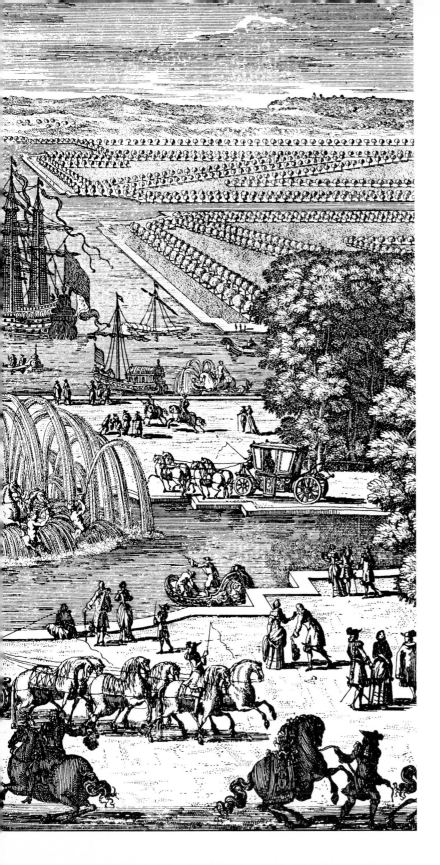

trees and flowers imported from all over the world, the canals rowed on by Venetian gondoliers, the mazes, avenues of topiary and garden sculpture, the open-air stages enclosed by high green hedges, the outdoor fêtes and firework displays – all this and more were the marvel and envy of every court in the world. It was said of the 'Sun King' that he had to create an art in harmony with his wide view of the universe, and with Versailles he certainly had.

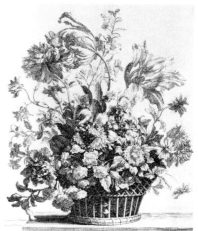

Basket of Flowers. Jean-Baptiste Monnoyer. French, 1634–99

In the engraving above, the artist has suggested the outline of a fountain with one group of flowers twisting gracefully upwards and others spilling over the edge of the basket. Jean-Baptiste Monnoyer was noted not only for his decorations at Versailles but also for those at the King's other residences.

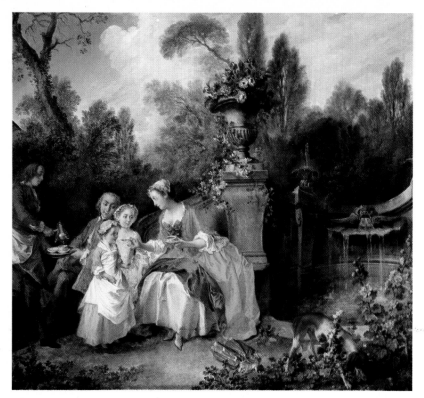

The Cup of Chocolate. Nicolas Lancret. French, 1690–1743

What lovelier background for a family portrait than a garden? This was especially true in the mid eighteenth century when women's clothes were as dainty and silken as flowers. It seems almost as if the lady prettily seated beside the urn at left had chosen her dress to match the flowers.

Nicolas Lancret was clever at thinking up something for his subjects to do while he painted them. As hot chocolate is served by the cool of the grotto at left, the mother holds out a teaspoon to give her youngest a taste, and below left, an elegant young couple occupy themselves outdoors with a game of backgammon while others watch.

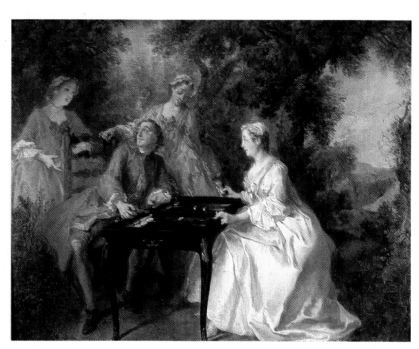

The Game of Backgammon. Nicolas Lancret. French, 1690–1743

Both Lancret and Antoine Watteau (who painted the picture at right) studied under Claude Gillot, director of theatrical costumes and design, and scene painter at the Paris Opéra. Gillot's deep interest in actors and acting influenced Watteau more than it did Lancret. To Watteau, it would seem, all the world became a stage, a glittering fairyland in which, it has been said, he saw 'women as goddesses and men as satyrs in fashionable clothes.' In his half real, half imagined dancing pavilion, Watteau bids us put on our fancy dress, join in with the music and dance the summer night through.

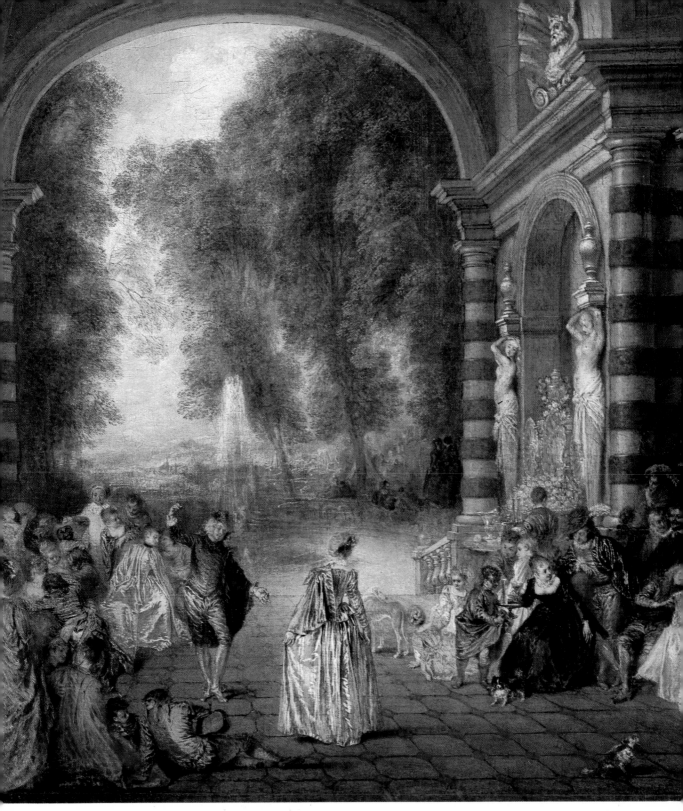

Pleasures of the Dance (detail). Antoine Watteau. French, 1684–1721

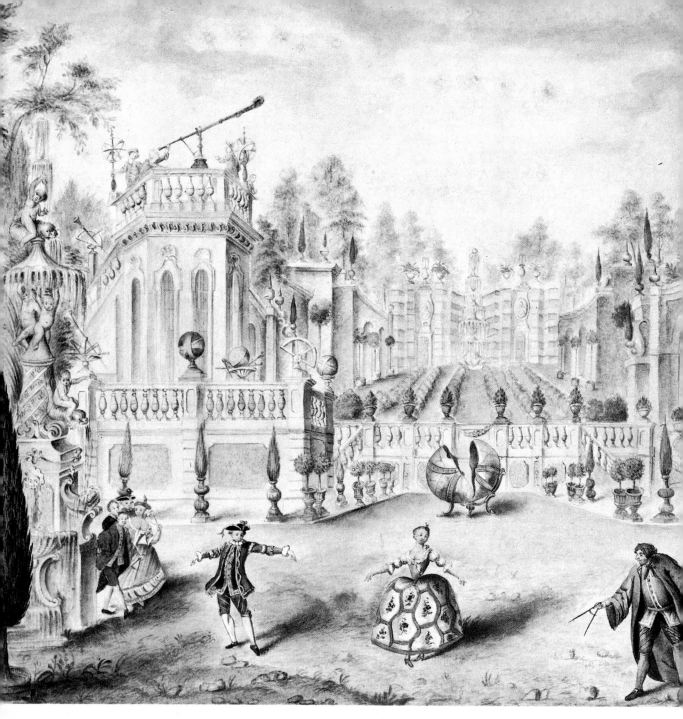

Ballets have been danced in the garden; more often, however, gardens have been the settings of ballets on stage. Here an astrologer, using his dividers, has just cracked open a large globe out of which has stepped the beautiful maiden who curtsies at the front of the stage before taking the hand of the handsome prince who waits to dance off with her. On the roof of the observatory, four young astrologers have just noticed – with astonishment, no doubt – that stars are shining

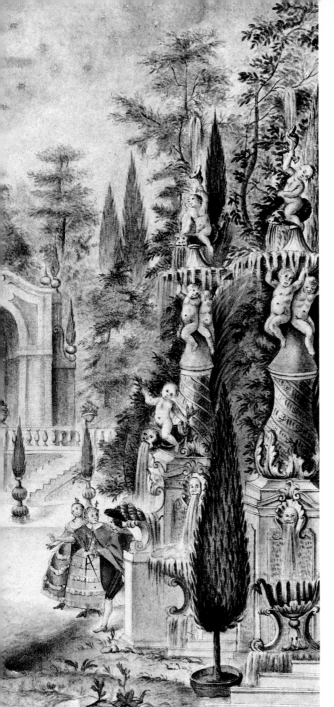

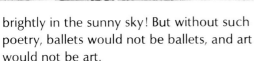

brightly in the sunny sky! But without such poetry, ballets would not be ballets, and art would not be art.

Eleanor Darnall. Justus Englehardt Kuhn.
American, 18th c.

The Astrologer's Garden,
stage set, c. 1780. Jean Georges Kopp

The young lady below lived not in Europe, as the background might suggest, but in America. However, the artist was born and trained in Europe and is known to have worked in Maryland between 1708 and 1717. If the large garden looks more 'old' world than 'new', the flowers are authentic. Roses, pinks and tulips were grown in America at this time.

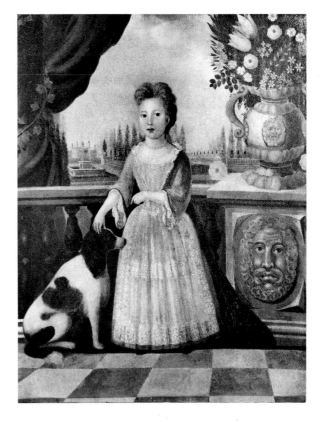

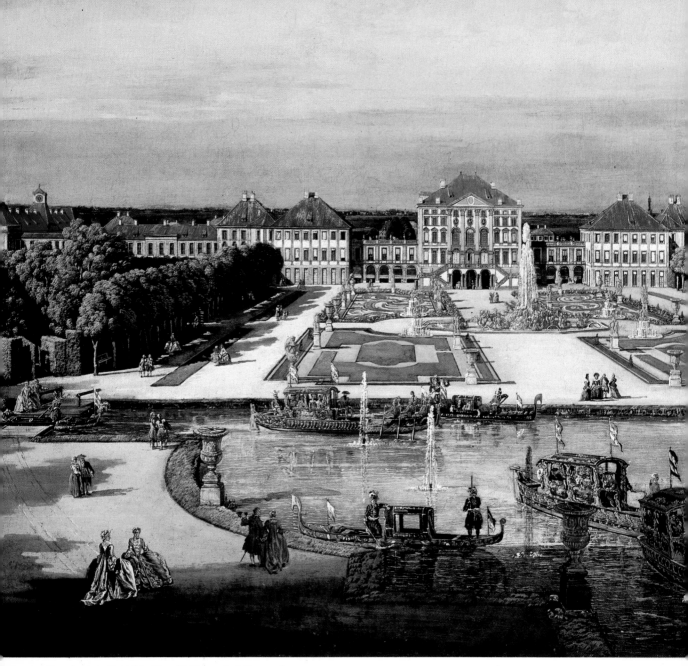

Nymphenburg Castle (detail), c. 1761. Bernardo Bellotto. Italian, 1720–80

The building of the magnificent castle and gardens at Nymphenburg, near Munich, was started in 1663, a year after work had begun at Versailles (pages 44–45). Additions were made in 1712, and this is how the summer residence of the Electors of Bavaria looked in about 1761. At that time,

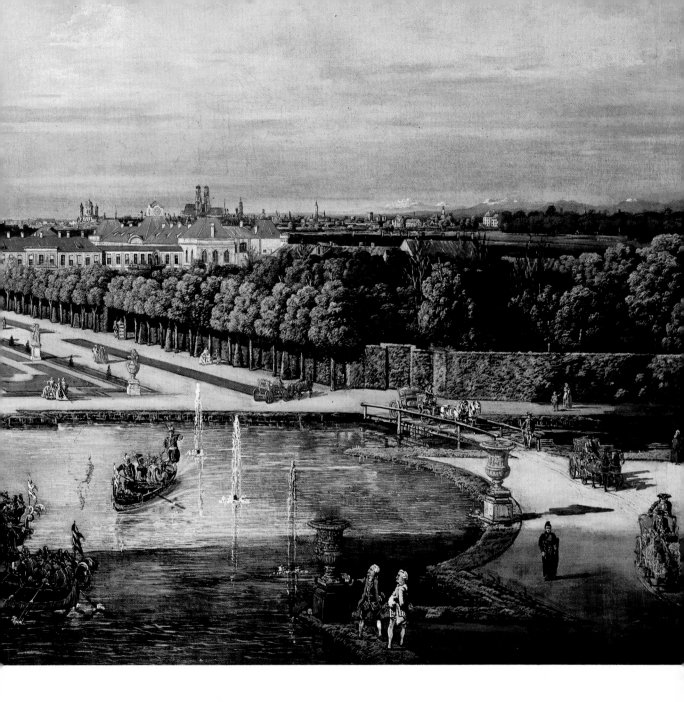

Bernardo Bellotto, the nephew and pupil of the great Venetian artist, Canaletto, was painting 'views' in and around Vienna and Munich and, judging from the activity here, must have thoroughly enjoyed this visit to Nymphenburg. A regatta appears to be in progress, as ornate gondolas packed with passengers and with flags flying are being rowed around, and in between, the splashing fountains. It was here at Nymphenburg that King Ludwig II was born in 1845, later to build dream palaces of his own, including Linderhof – on page 78.

The outsize swan in the engraving below is not, of course, a real bird – it's a pleasure boat, shaped like a swan, in which King George III (1738–1820) sailed up the Thames from London to enjoy the new gardens at Kew. These had been founded in 1761, and are an example of the so-called 'landscaped garden' which had lately been introduced by William Kent, Philip Southcote, Charles Bridgeman, Lancelot 'Capability' Brown and other noted architects who turned English garden design upside down. 'Nature abhors a straight line,' said Kent, so instead of building walled-in enclosures like those of medieval gardens, or using the traditional geometric designs – as seen on the last two pages – these gentlemen tossed their rulers and compasses to the winds. In their hands, the garden became a wide open park with sweeping expanses of smooth lawn, sinuous paths and walks leading down to a natural looking lake, pond or river in which a lordly mansion, pavilion, temple, clump of shrubbery or trees would be reflected in a highly picturesque way.

The Bathing Pool at right is by Hubert Robert, whom the French nicknamed 'Robert of the Ruins' because after his visit to Rome in 1754 Robert dreamed of nothing else but romantic landscapes with crumbling architecture and pretty figures like these ladies taking a dip at the foot of a domeless rotunda. The new fashion for classical architecture – in America as in Europe – followed the unearthing in 1748 of the Roman city of Pompeii, which had been buried since the eruption of Vesuvius in AD 79.

The Bathing Pool (detail), 1777–84.
Hubert Robert. French, 1733–1808

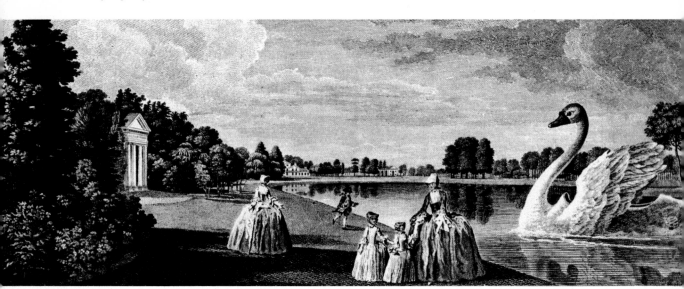

Swan at Kew Gardens. Engraving. William Woollett. 18th c.

Overleaf: The idea of a garden as a place for young people to enjoy every sort of game – from blindman's buff and hide-and-seek to swings and kissing games – appealed to Honoré Fragonard as much as it had to his teacher François Boucher, the master of this 'rococo' style of painting. Fragonard's formal garden landscape, on the next two pages, with its flowery vistas, pretty faces and elegant clothes, reflects the taste of the French aristocracy in those last carefree days before the revolution brought the downfall of the monarchy.

Blindman's Buff (detail), c. 1765. Jean-Honoré Fragonard. French, 1732–1806

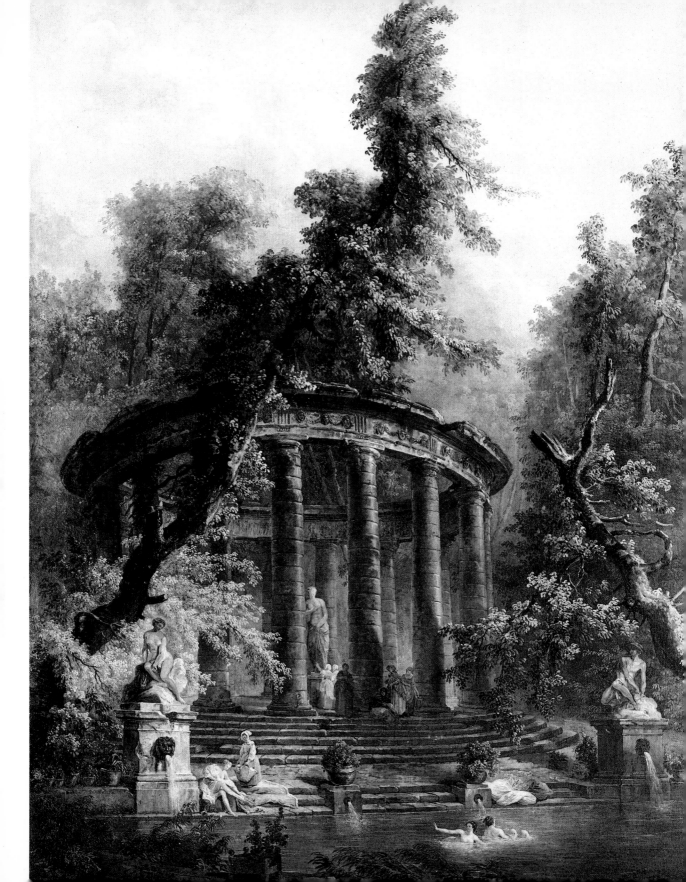

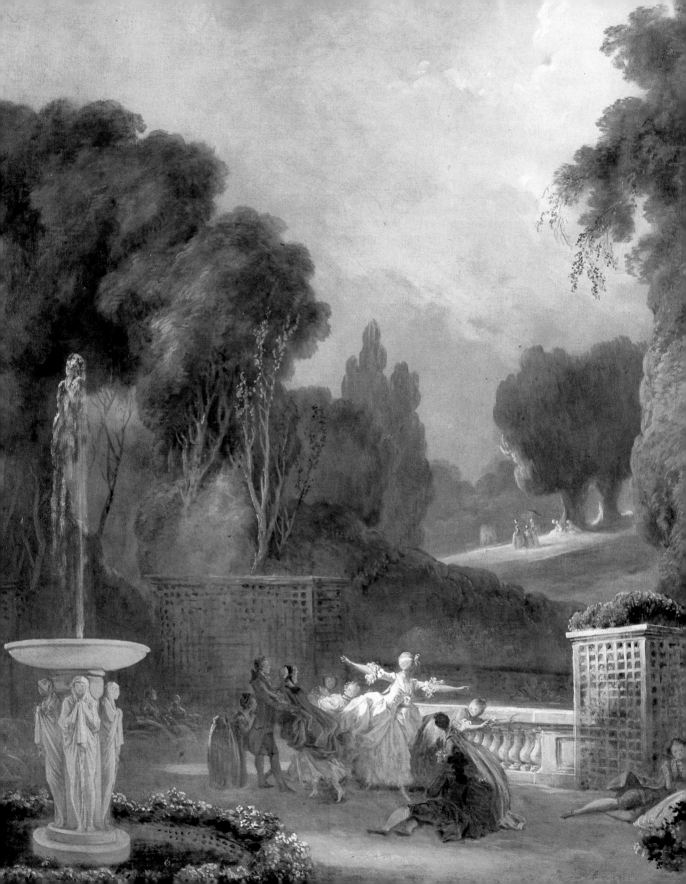

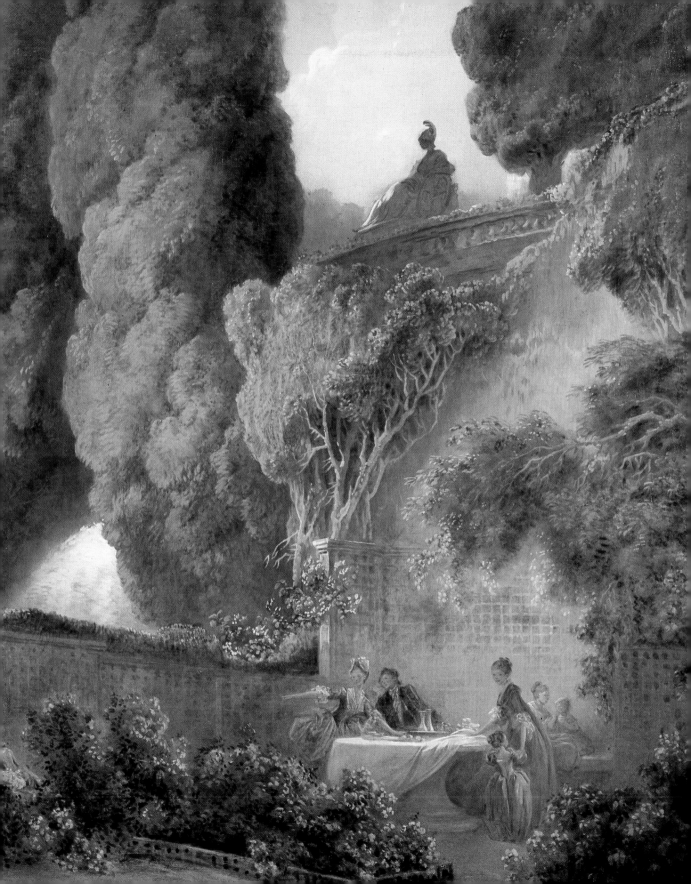

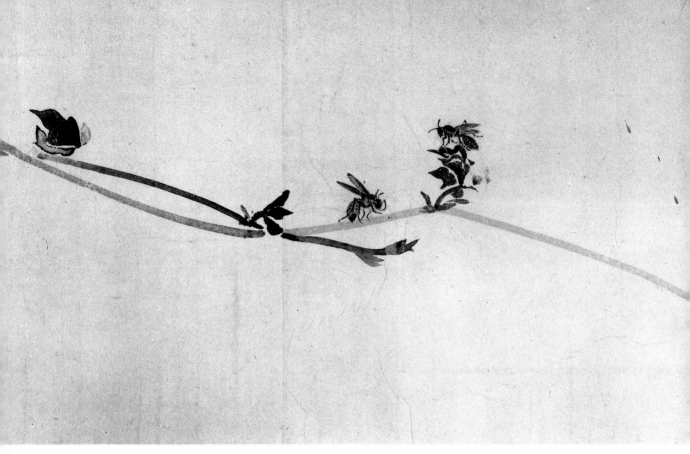

Flowers of the Seasons (detail). Mori Sosen. Japanese, 1747–1821

While European artists – like Fragonard (pages 54–55) – enjoyed painting trees, shrubbery and flowers in profusion, the oriental artist took greater delight in painting one or two details at a time. Individual blossoms on a branch, as above, were to be enjoyed for the beauty of every petal, every leaf. Even a stem of jasmine, here offering two wasps a taste of nectar, was worth a drawing for its graceful curve alone.

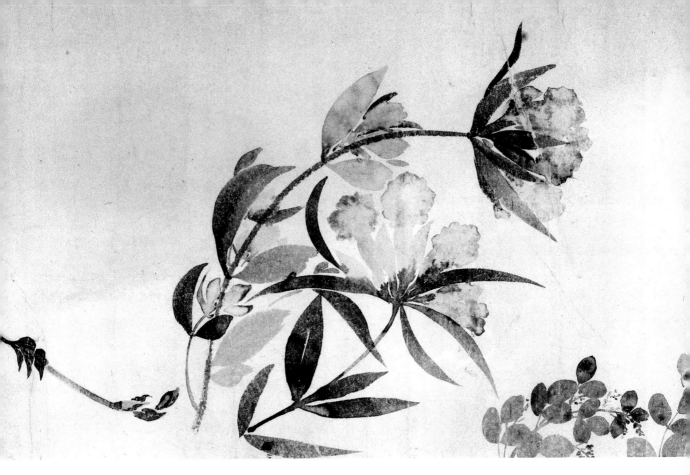

Cat and Butterfly (detail).
Hand-scroll. Katsushika Hokusai.
Japanese, 1760–1849

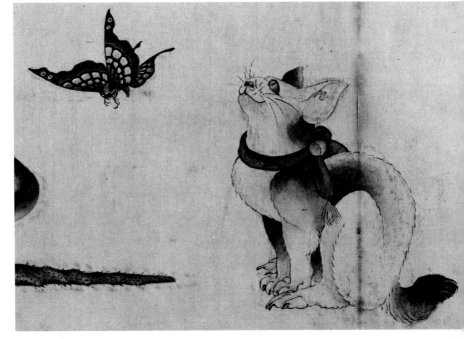

Hokusai singled out the cat and
butterfly at right, leaving the
background of a Japanese garden
entirely to our imagination. He
also makes us wonder how long
the butterfly will remain safe
from the cat who wears such a
very self-satisfied smile.

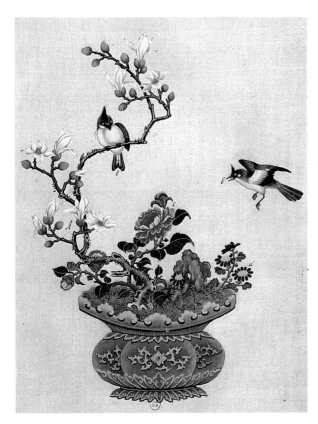

Flowers and Birds. Chinese painting on silk. Late 18th c.

The Chinese have always delighted the West with paintings in which they have twisted nature just a little this way or that to gain a more decorative effect. Here a flowering branch arranged in a fancy urn was made to resemble a real tree by the suggestion of a flower bed at its base and the addition of the two birds.

Bird fanciers have sometimes built aviaries to resemble small temples, giving plenty of room for the birds as well as adding interest to a large garden. This design, with a touch of the Chinese, was for a pheasantry. As trade increased with the Far East in the eighteenth century, ships returning to Europe and America were filled with exotic objects that inspired local designers to make imitations. This resulted in a style known as 'chinoiserie'.

58   Design for a pheasantry at the Royal Pavilion, Brighton, 1808. Engraving. Humphrey Repton. English, 1725–1818

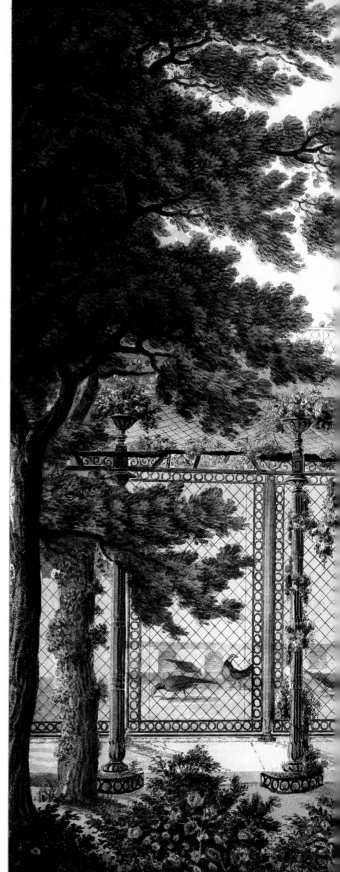

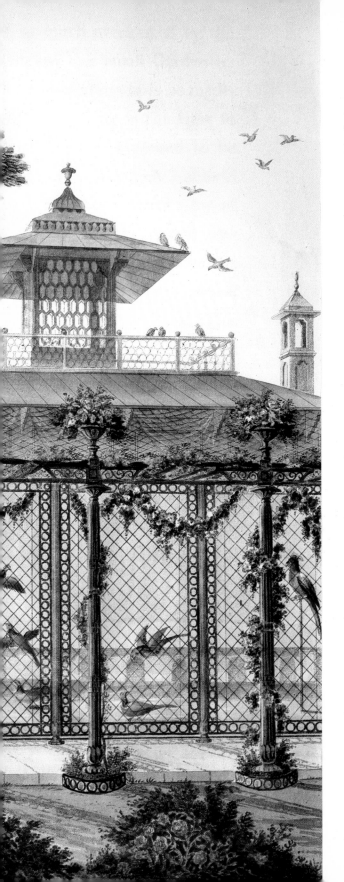

A happy looking dog in a garden. Early in the eighteenth century, the Italian court painter, Giuseppe Castiglione, became a Jesuit missionary to China, where he adopted the Chinese way of painting.

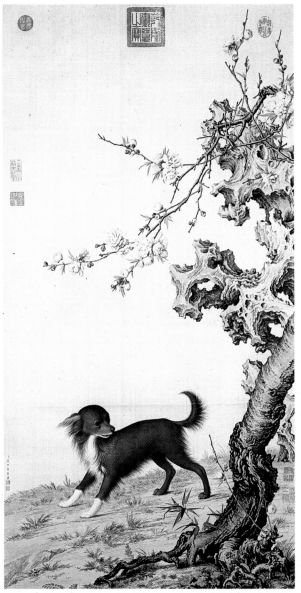

Dog under Flowering Branches. Giuseppe Castiglione. Italian, 1688–1766

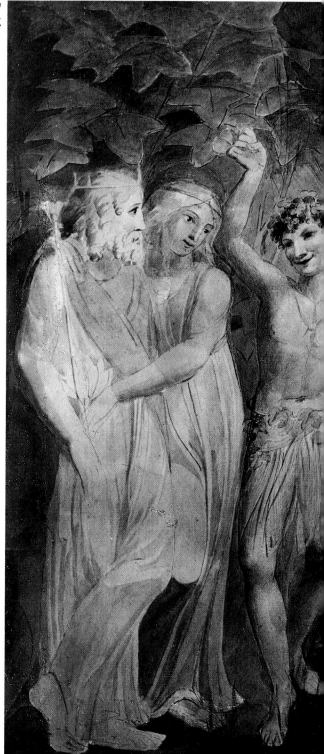

Oberon, Titania and Puck with
Fairies Dancing, c. 1785–90.
William Blake. English, 1757–1827

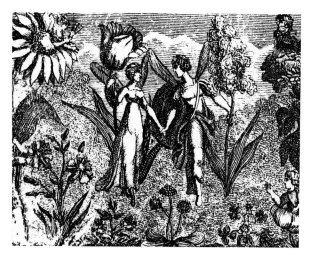

Hyacinth and Tulip. Charles. Engraving. 18th–19th c.

Fairies are always believed to live in woods and
dells and to hide themselves in gardens. Bearing
a tulip and a hyacinth, these two were very likely
on their way to a butterfly's ball.

One occasion when everyone can be convinced
of the existence of these charming and busy little
people is at a stage performance of *A Midsummer
Night's Dream*. At right, William Blake, the artist
and poet who claimed to have enjoyed 'regular
visits from heavenly emissaries', has painted
Shakespeare's fairies at their midnight revels.
While some of them, wearing butterfly wings and
headdresses of flowers, dance lightly round their
fairy ring, the mischievous Puck tries to attract the
attention of Oberon, their King, and Queen
Titania.

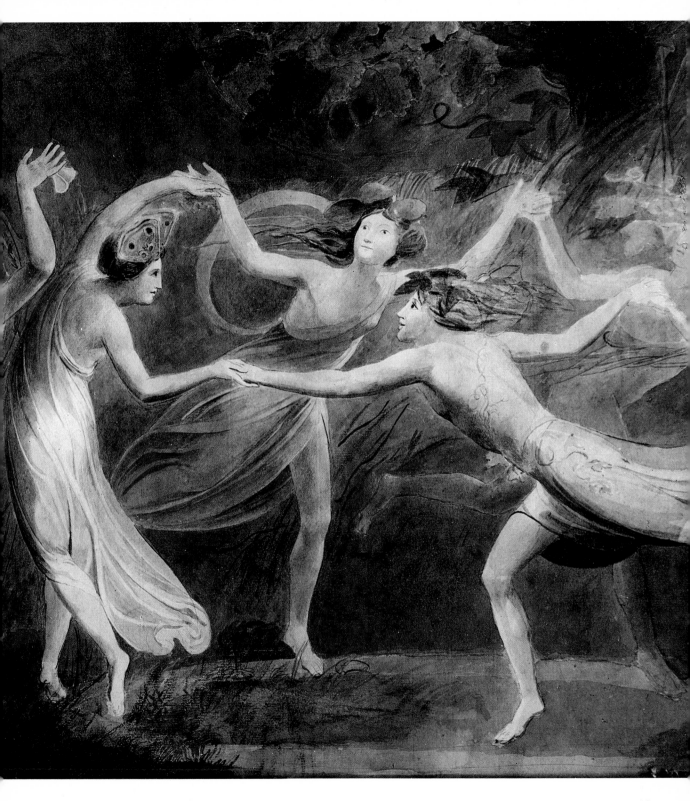

The sunny scene at right shows the garden as a playground, as a place for a sit-down chat and as a pleasant spot for reading. But by including the gardener with his wheelbarrow the artist reminds us that beautiful gardens don't remain beautiful unless someone gets on with the work.

It seems possible that the scarcity of flowers in winter one day gave some potter the idea of making a vase as pretty as a summer bouquet so that it could be used to decorate a table instead of real flowers. This example was made at England's Bow factory in 1760.

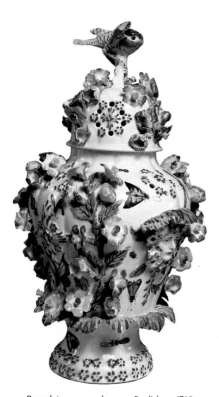

Porcelain vase and cover. English, c. 1760

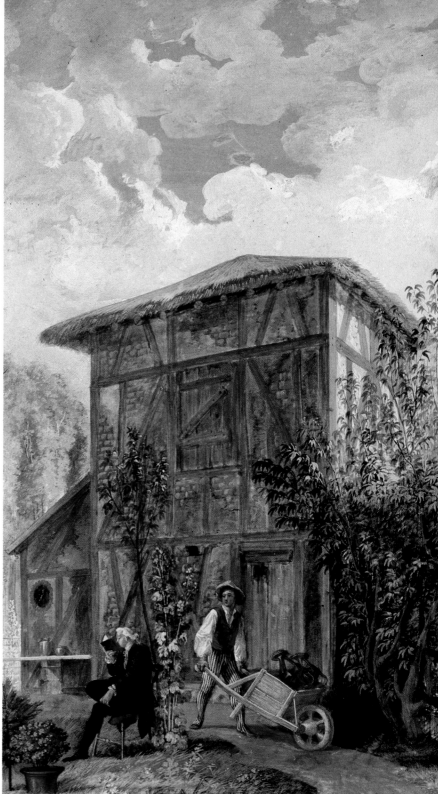

Playground in a Garden. Jean-Demosthène Dugourc. French, 1749–1825

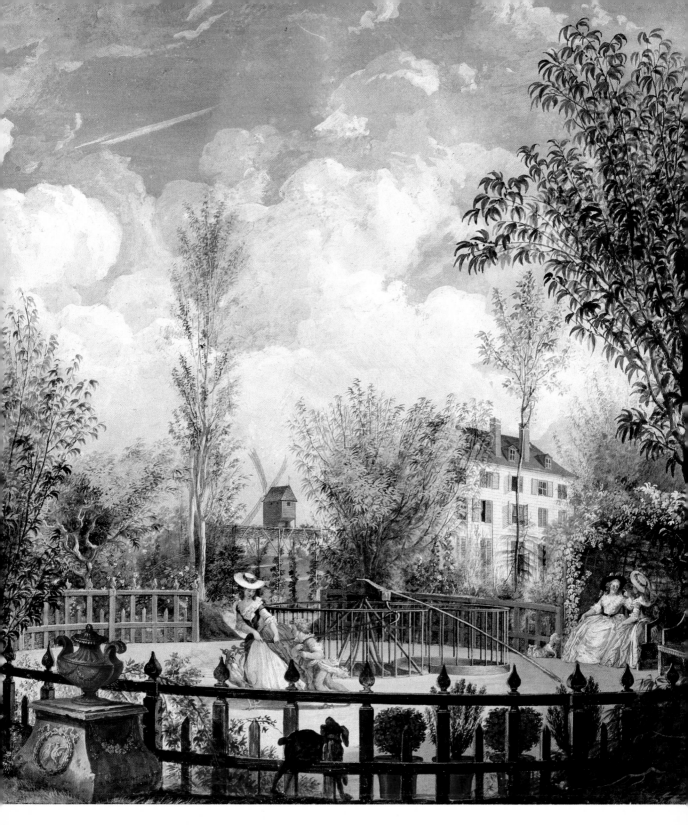

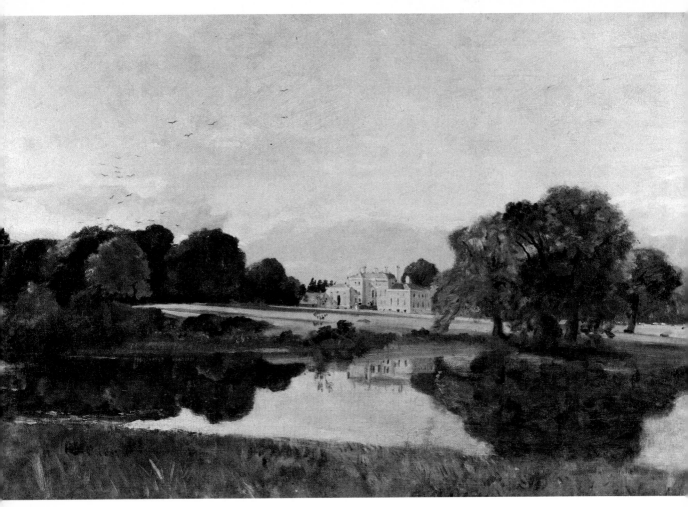

Malvern Hall, Warwickshire, 1809. John Constable. English, 1776–1837

This private park, with casual groupings of trees and grasslands leading to an irregular shaped lake in which the stately Malvern Hall is reflected, was painted by John Constable during his visit to Warwickshire in 1809. (The hall is now a private school for boys.) This is the kind of view that the handsome young couple in Thomas Gainsborough's portrait at right would have had on their morning walk some twenty-four years earlier. William and Elizabeth Hallet, both twenty-one and just married, walk arm in arm along 'a garden avenue with venerable shade' accompanied by their pet spitz. This has been called 'the most poetic portrait England's greatest portrait painter ever made.'

Morning Walk, 1785.
Thomas Gainsborough. English, 1727–88

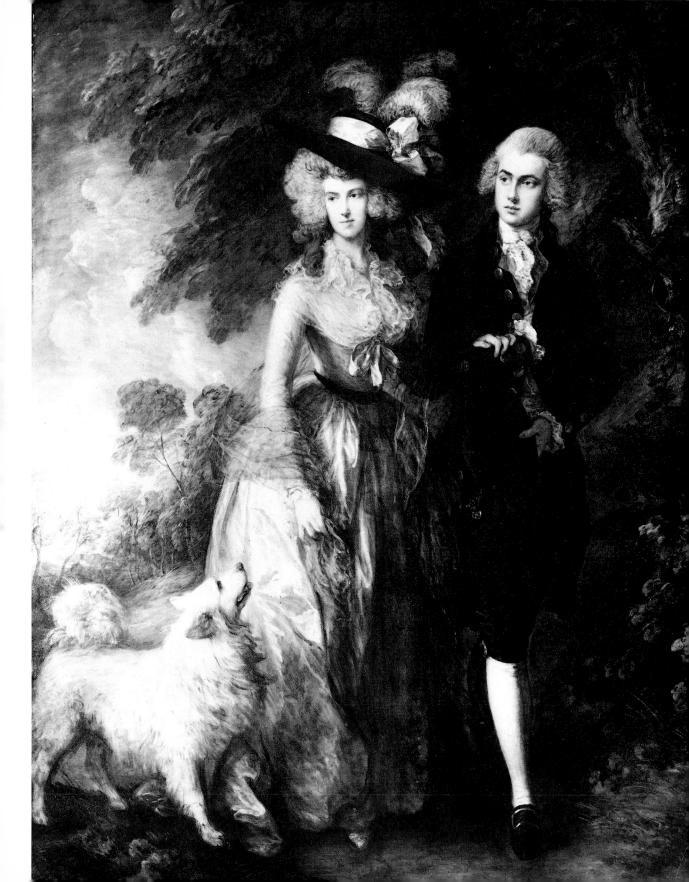

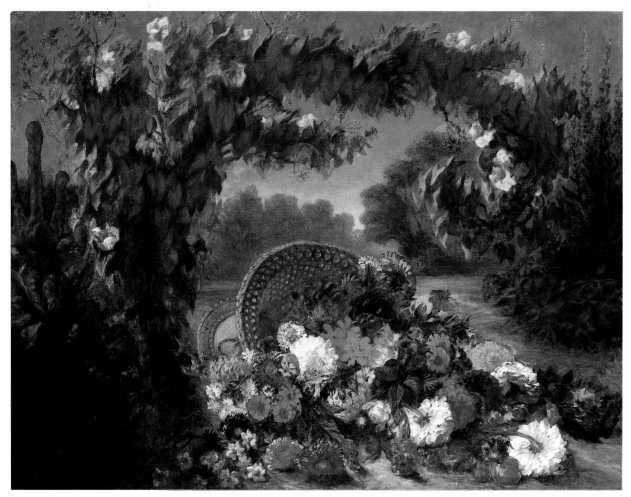

Basket of Flowers, 1848–49. Eugène Delacroix. French, 1798–1863

Instead of arranging flowers upright in a basket, Eugène Delacroix was poet enough to paint masses of them tumbling onto the ground. The curling branch above suggests the twisting movement of wind which could have blown the basket over.

To many people, a garden without a bird would be a garden without a spirit. Winging down from the sky to alight on a tree, dropping to the lawn and hopping back onto a branch and singing, birds fill the garden with unending movement and delight. At far right are Audubon's yellow-breasted chats.

Less of a pet, because it competes for our vegetables, is the gentle rabbit.

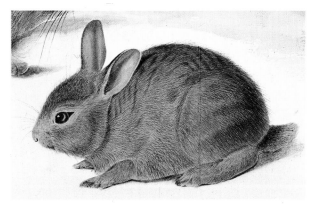

Gray Rabbit, 1785. John James Audubon. American, 1780–1851

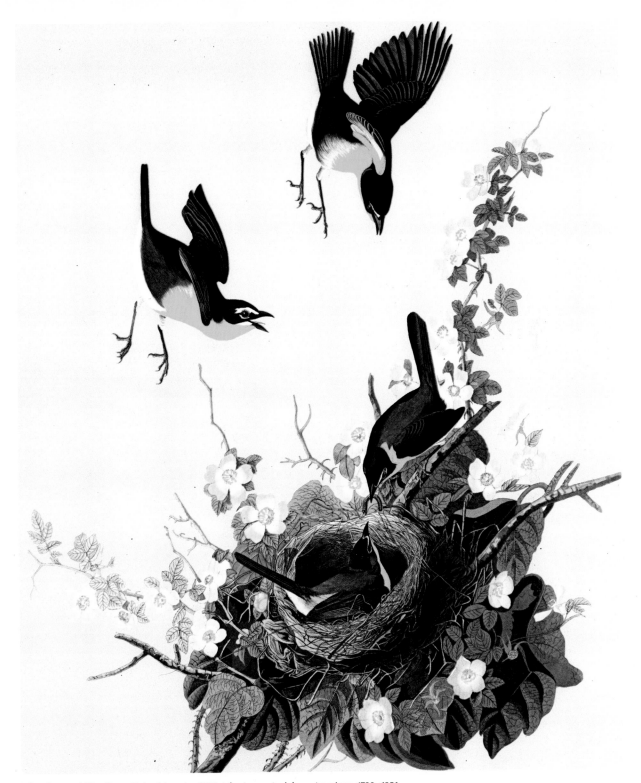

Yellow-breasted Chat. From *Birds of America*, 1838. John James Audubon. American, 1780–1851

The thatched cottage at Sidmouth in English Regency style, with its garden, was started by Lord Despencer in 1805 and was finished, as at right, by Thomas L. Fish, in 1818. In the foreground are two peacocks, those 'travelling gardens of iridescence', which continued to be popular until World War I, when gardens became smaller and smaller because of the high cost of owning and maintaining them.

A lady in a rose garden wearing lilies on her head and bows on her toes. The pagoda shaped dress, fringed with tassels, is an example of 'chinoiserie' – a style which continued to be fashionable into the nineteenth century.

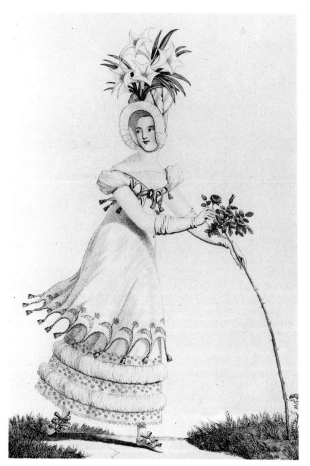

Lady Wearing an Italian Straw Hat and a Chinese-style Wrap, c. 1815. Horace Vernet. French, 1789–1863

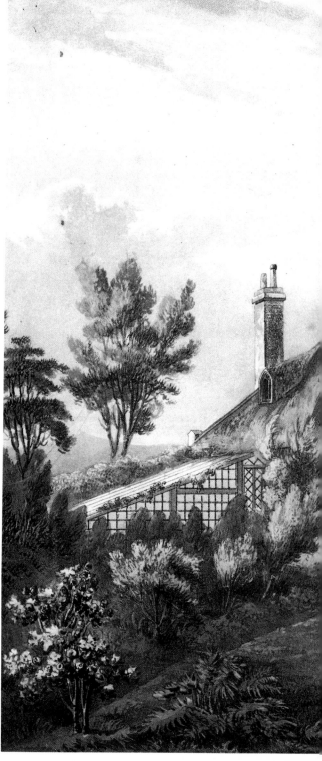

View of Knowle Cottage, Sidmouth, c. 1818. Aquatint. English

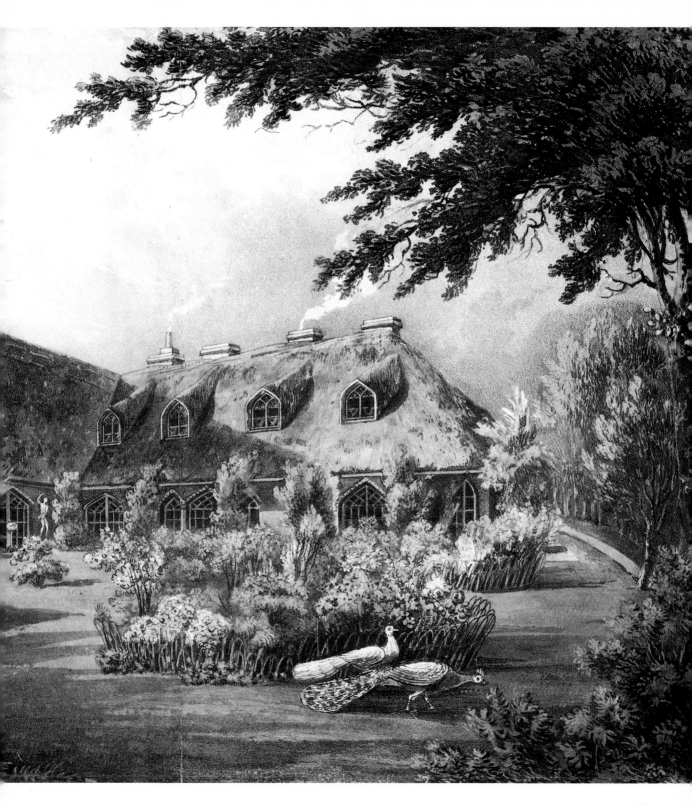

69

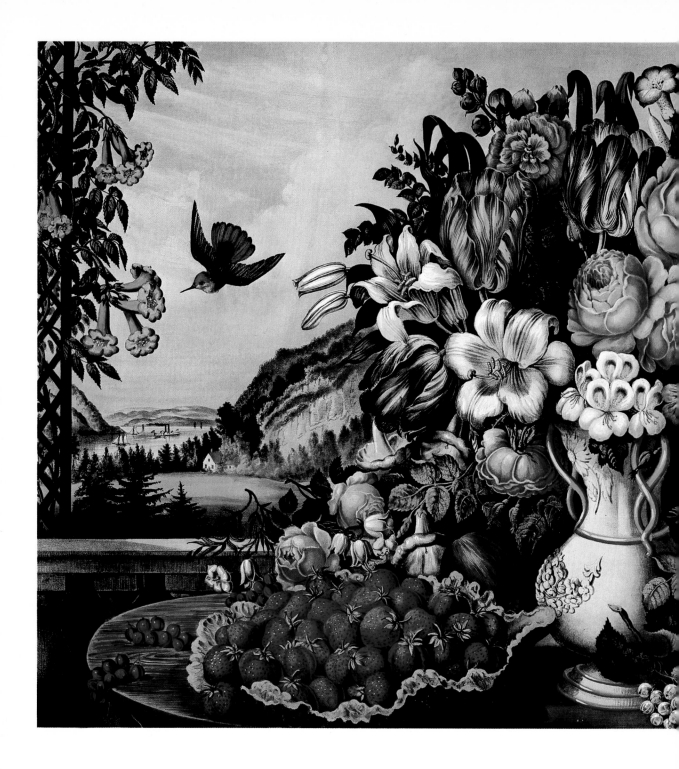

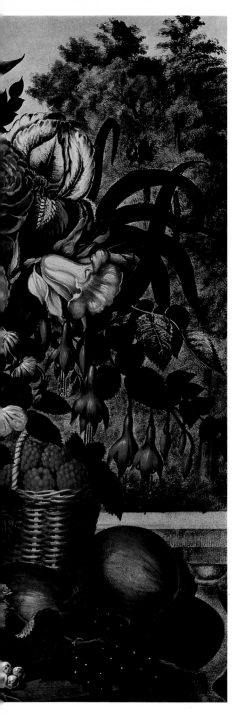

The joys of owning a strawberry patch, raspberry canes and grapevines, in addition to beds of flowers, are temptingly suggested in the lithograph made after the painting of 1862 by Fanny Palmer. A humming-bird hovers beside the trumpet-vine, and across the garden and field our eyes are led down the steep slope to the river on which sailboats sail and a steamboat paddles off into the distance.

The charming little girl below picks another rose for her beadwork basket, as her kitten runs to welcome her.

Landscape, Fruit and Flowers, 1862. Hand-coloured lithograph by Currier & Ives, from painting by Fanny Palmer. American, 19th c.

Little Girl, c. 1840. John Bradley. American, 19th c.

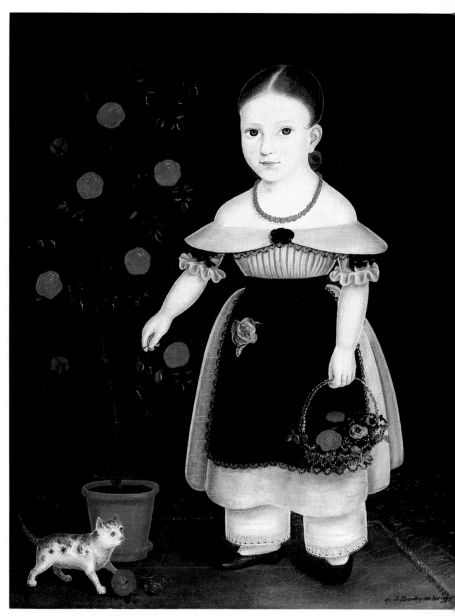

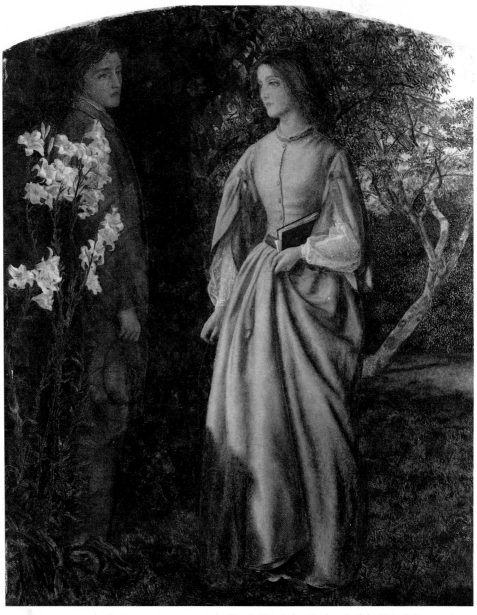

Aurora Leigh's Dismissal of Romney (The Tryst), 1860. Arthur Hughes. English, 1830–1915

Bitter-sweet moments can take place in the garden too. As the image of her suitor fades into the shadow of the tree, Aurora's gaze is held by the bright lilies which, perhaps, will always remind her of this farewell tryst. Romance and nostalgia were popular among the Pre-Raphaelite artists – the new movement Arthur Hughes had joined in 1850. At right, drama raises its head in the shape of an unfaithful lover – just visible above the fence – dangling a flower and smiling sweetly at the rival of an earlier sweetheart who places her hand over an aching heart.

Broken Vows, 1856.
Philip Hermogenes Calderon.
English, 1833–98

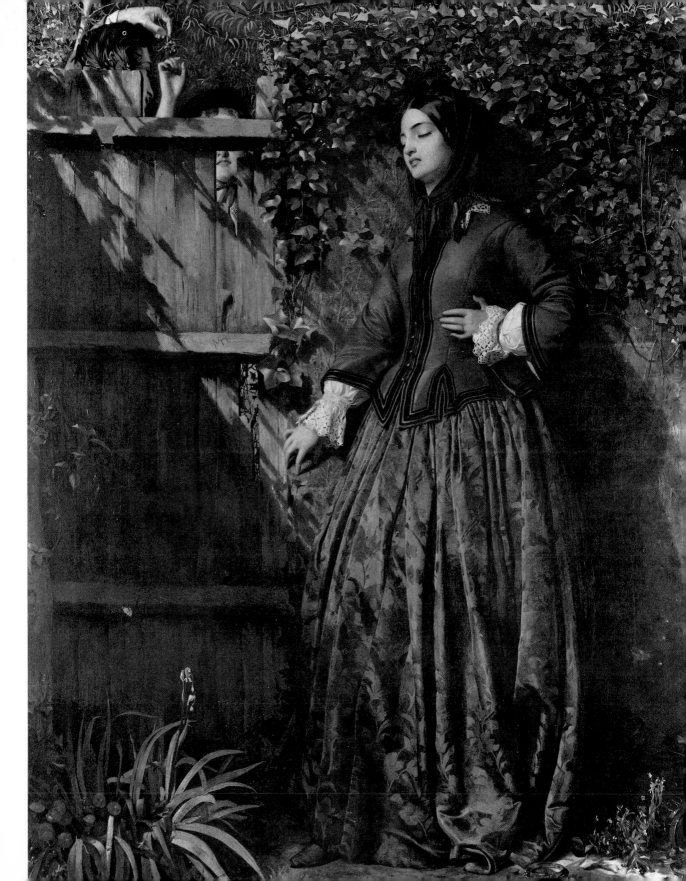

It was for her unrequited love of Hamlet that Ophelia lost her mind and, after gathering masses of flowers between the garden and river bank, was finally to fall into the brook and drown. In Millais' interpretation of this moment in Shakespeare's tragedy, Ophelia clutches a single flower as the others cling to her dress, which slowly drags her down.

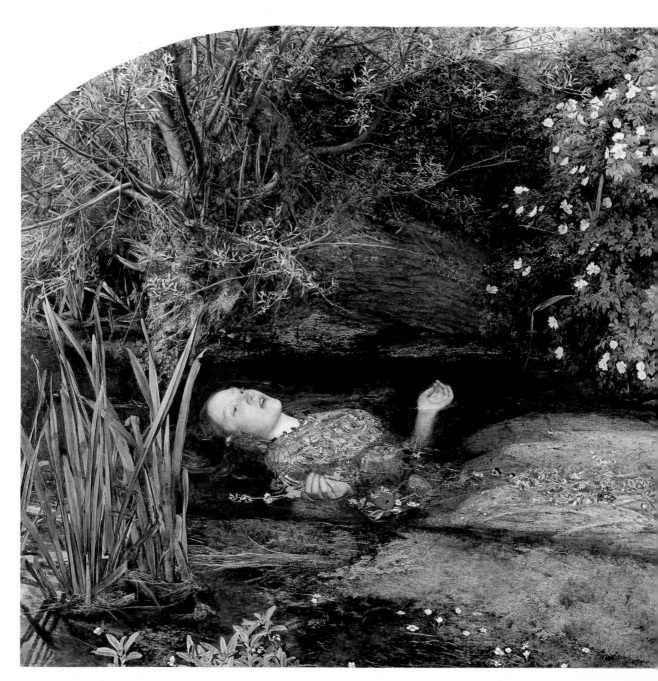

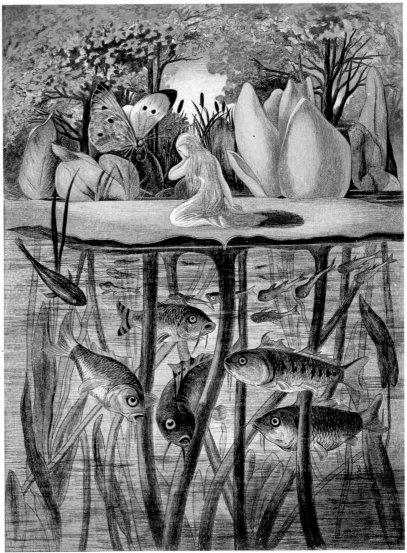

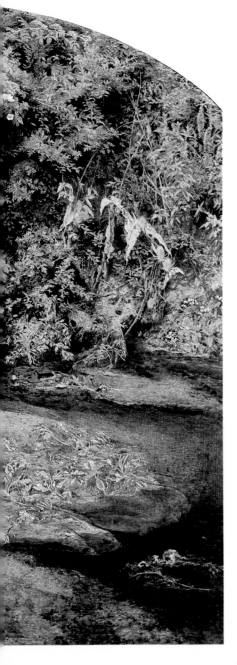

A kinder fate awaits the heroine of Hans Andersen's fairytale, Thumbelina, seated here on the broad leaf of a water-lily weeping at the prospect of marrying the ugly toad's son. The fishes come to her rescue, nibbling at the stem so the leaf starts floating downstream and bears her away to foreign lands. Eventually, after a ride on a swallow's back, Thumbelina meets and marries a prince of her own size and the two live happily ever after.

The 'human' rose, queen of flowers, surrounded by adoring beetles below, and the narcissus on the opposite page admiring her reflection, are by Grandville. In 1829, this French artist had a book published in which animals were seen dressed and behaving like humans – an idea that illustrators of children's books have been imitating ever since. Grandville again surprised the world in 1847 with his book, 'The Animated Flowers', from which these two drawings are taken.

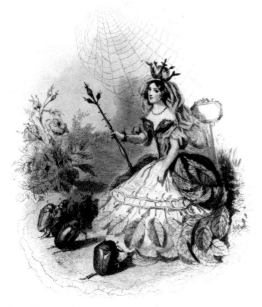

Rose. From *Les Fleurs animées*. Grandville. French, 1803–47

The scene at the end of the garden, at right, is from *Lohengrin*, the ancient German fairytale that Richard Wagner made into an opera in 1848. Lohengrin, standing on the bank of the river Schelde with the castle of the Holy Grail in the background, has been sent for to save the

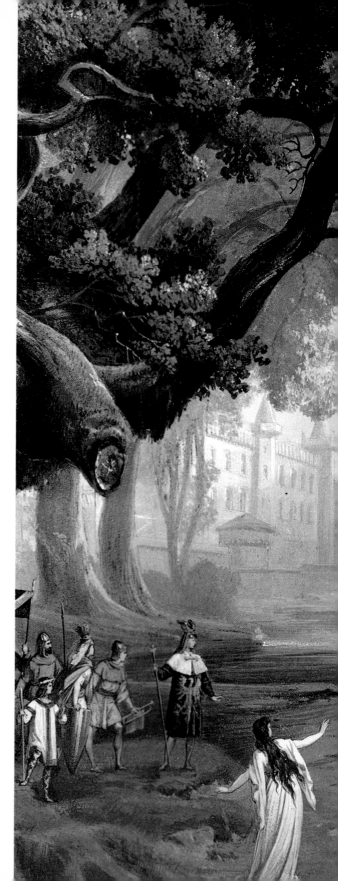

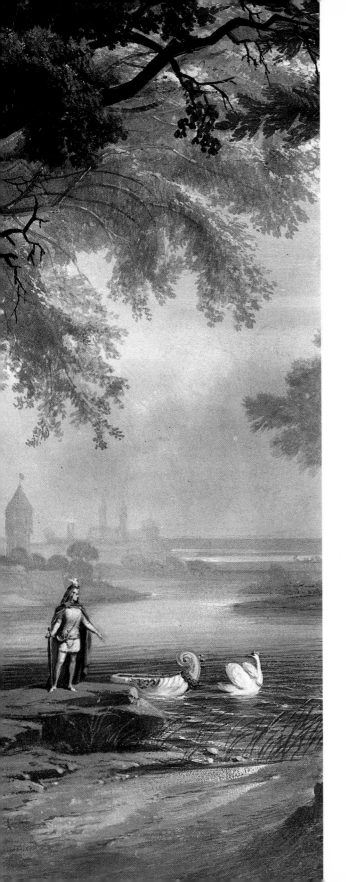

Princess Elsa of Brabant from an undesirable suitor. The swan – who reappears later in the story, revealing himself in true fairytale manner as the brother of Elsa – is seen here about to draw Lohengrin in a boat down the Schelde to Antwerp where Lohengrin eventually saves Elsa and marries her. 'Who could possibly remain unmoved by this magical fairytale, by this heavenly music?' cried King Ludwig II, the 'Dream King' of Bavaria who built the palace which appears on the next page.

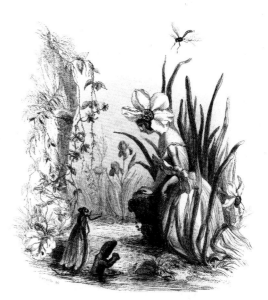

Narcissus. From *Les Fleurs animées.* Grandville. French, 1803–47

Design for Wagner's
Lohengrin (detail), 1868.
Heinrich Döll. German, 19th c.

Whenever Ludwig II stayed at Linderhof, he enjoyed looking across the formal French garden to the pond with its jet rising nearly a hundred feet high, and watching the swans. They reminded him of *Lohengrin* (as on the last page), the opera he had first seen in 1861 at the age of sixteen. So inspired was Ludwig by all Wagner's operas that later on, when the composer fell on hard times, he became his enthusiastic sponsor and close friend. Wagner's music contributed to the romantic dreams that led the king to build his fairytale palaces and castles – four in all.

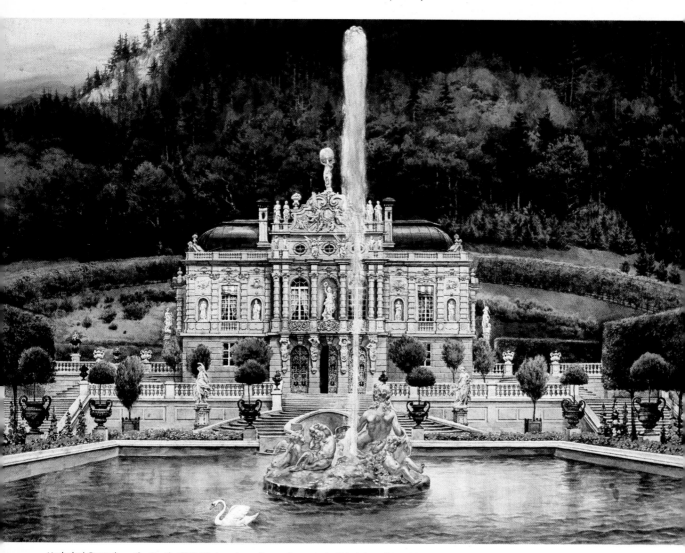

Linderhof Castle from the South, 1882. Watercolour after a photograph. Heinrich Brelling. German, 19th c.

At right, the majestic figure framed by spring blossoms was painted by Samuel Palmer who was already exhibiting at London's Royal Academy at the age of fifteen. In 1824, Palmer met and became the disciple of William Blake (pages 60–61) whose influence explains in part the quiet air of mystery and magic that envelops this garden in Kent's Shoreham valley.

In a Shoreham Garden. Samuel Palmer. English, 1805–81

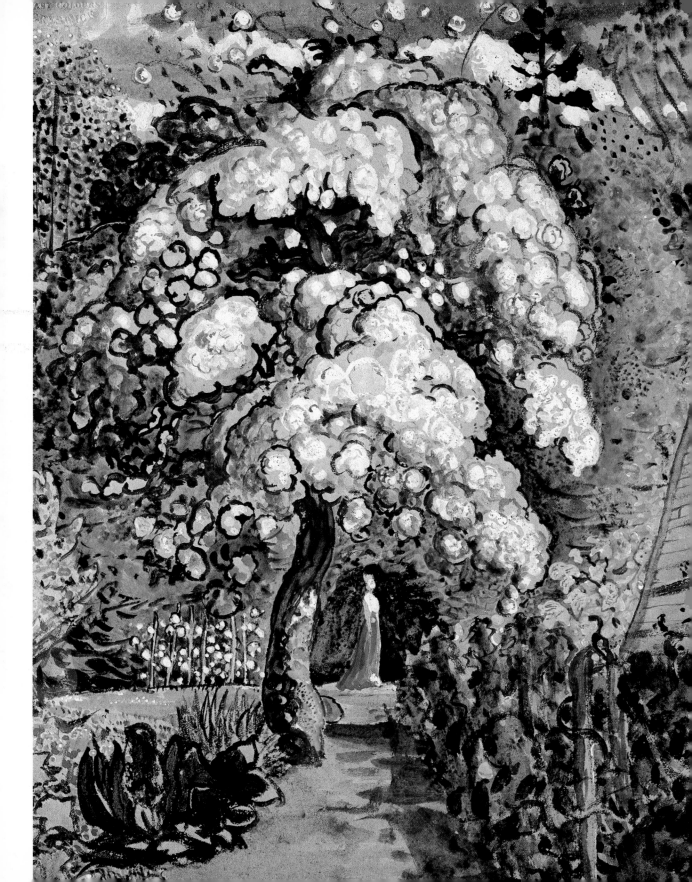

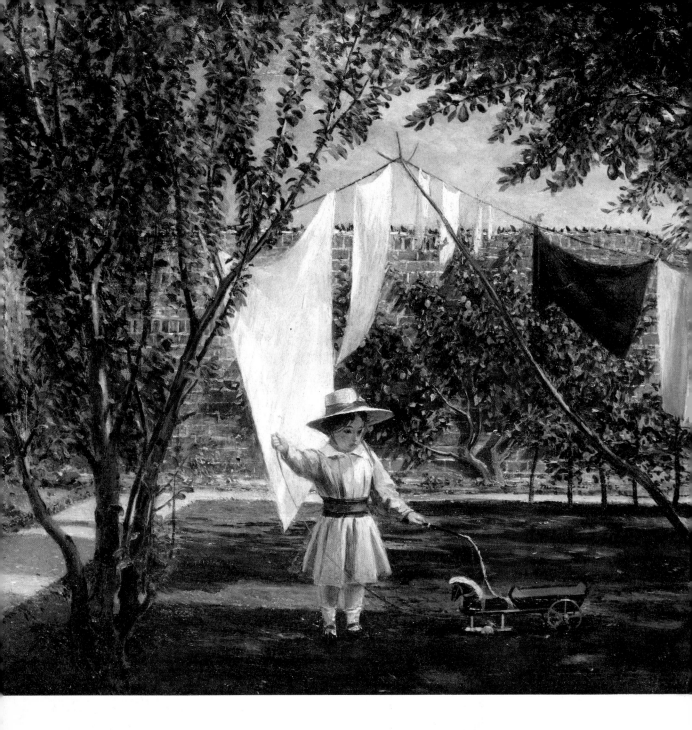

This child's world is a small world where a lawn is the size of a parkland, a vast expanse of green through which a horse and carriage is about to be pulled round and up a hidden driveway to a mansion of his dreams. And the sheets on the line? Seen through half closed eyes, one moment they might be sails on sailboats, the next flags fluttering above a castle wall.

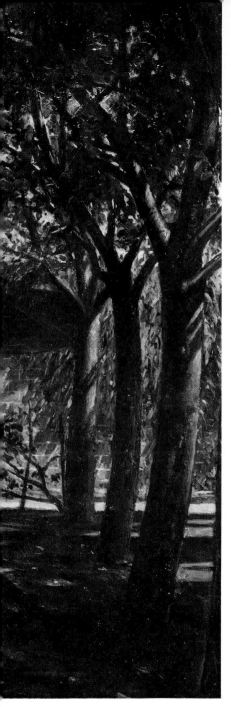

For the little girl below, the garden may be no more than a wall in which a few sunflowers have seeded themselves. Yet there's a friendly bird always waiting to be talked to and fed, there's a field below with trees to climb, and a path lined with wild flowers, some to be gathered for the table, some for her hair.

A Garden Scene, 1840. Charles Robert Leslie. English, 1794–1859

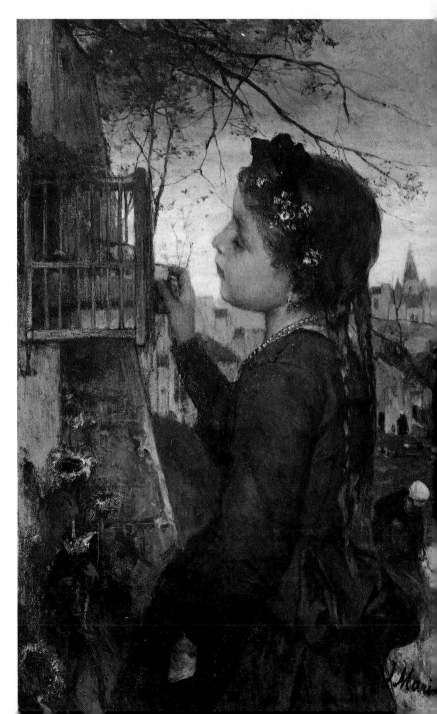

A Girl Feeding a Bird in a Cage, c. 1867. Jacobus Hendricus Maris. Dutch, 1837–99

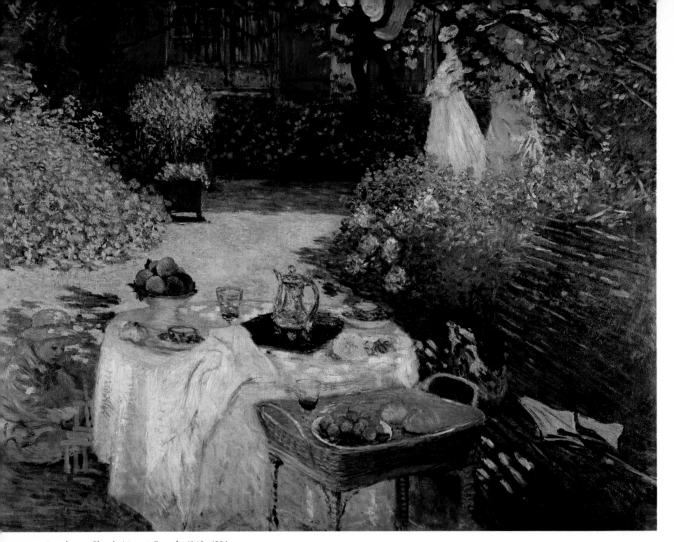

Luncheon. Claude Monet. French, 1840–1926

Lunch is over, and as the ladies return from a stroll around the garden the child is still happily building his house. To show what was served for lunch, Claude Monet painted a touch of wine in the glasses on the table, a coffee pot with cups and some unfinished rolls and fruit.

The scene at right was also painted by Monet when he was a struggling artist of twenty-five. With hardly enough money to pay a single model to pose for him, let alone four, he asked a girl named Camille to take each of the four positions around the tree so he could paint them in turn and thus complete the picture he had in mind. Monet's great passion as a painter was light, and although only one or two fellow artists appreciated his atmospheric, fleeting or 'impressionistic' way of painting at the time, few canvases in today's market are likely to fetch a higher price than a garden by Monet.

Women in a Garden. Claude Monet. French, 1840–1926

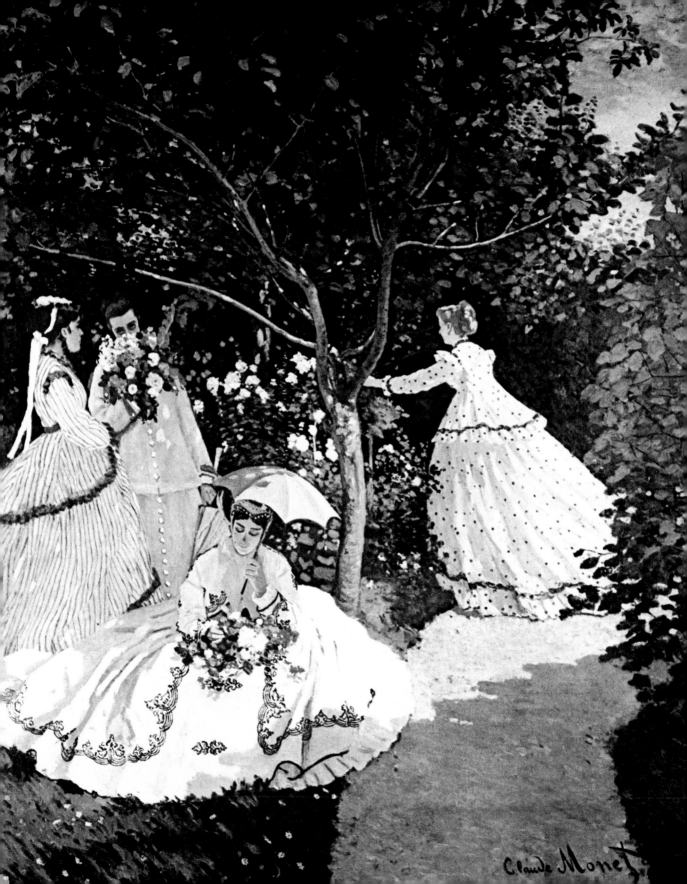

Dressing up – as at right – for a picnic in Victorian times required that the food be just as elegantly prepared and served. After bringing the kettle to the boil and making tea, one of the ladies adds a drop of milk to the cup of the lazy young man who is taking both her service, and her smile, quite for granted.

The two little girls below, opening Japanese lanterns to hang up for a garden party, brought immediate fame to the American born artist John Singer Sargent when this painting hung in the Royal Academy in 1887 and was purchased for the English nation. Sargent, who came to England in 1884, stayed on to become the most fashionable portrait painter of his day.

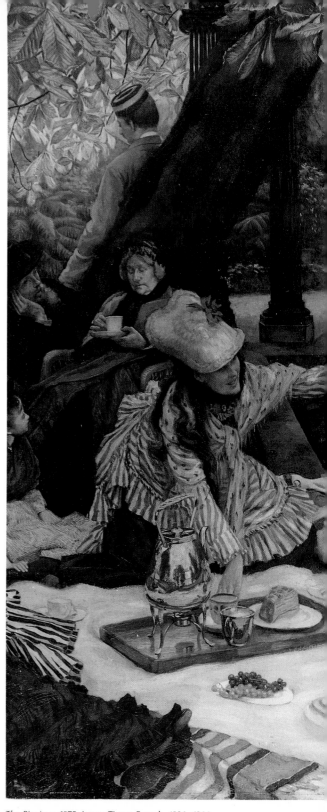

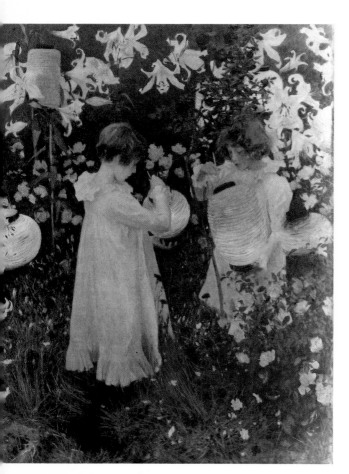

Carnation, Lily, Lily, Rose, 1883–86. John Singer Sargent. American, 1856–1925

The Picnic, c. 1875. James Tissot. French, 1836–1902

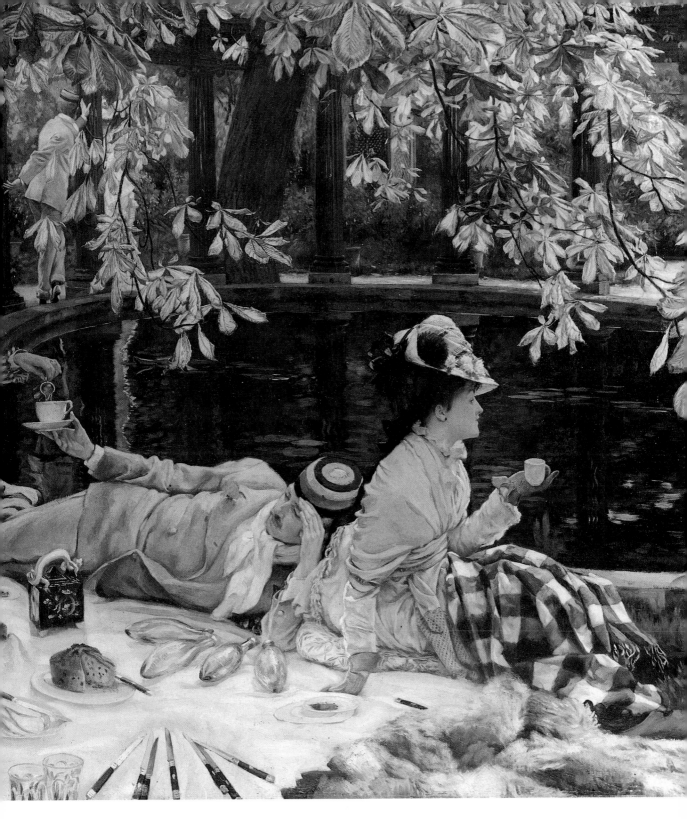

The terrace at right, radiant with geraniums, nasturtiums and gladioli, and looking out across the busy English Channel, was painted at the French summer resort of Sainte-Adresse. Breezy as the day was, it wasn't too windy for the ladies to put up their parasols – which helped Monet both with his composition and to emphasize the feeling of a bright sunny day at the seaside.

The sight of this little girl, with a watering-can to match her size, must have so delighted Auguste Renoir – who adored children – that he asked her to pose for him. Renoir, like his fellow Impressionist painter Monet, loved 'joyous and pretty things' and filled his canvases with light and shade and such bright hues that it was almost as if the sun itself had touched the tip of his brush.

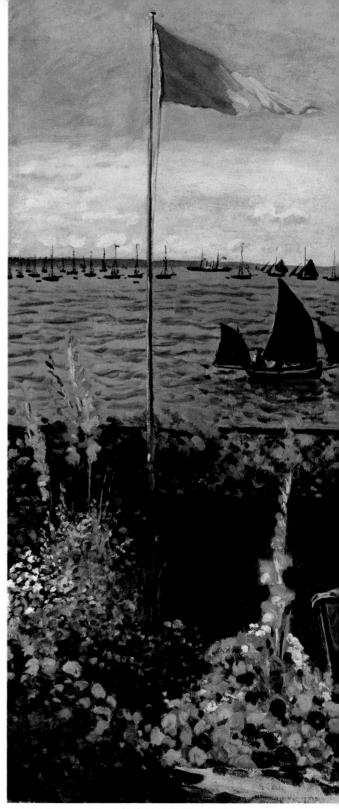

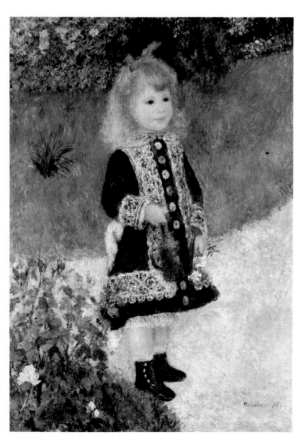

Girl with a Watering-can, 1876. Auguste Renoir. French, 1841–1919

Terrace at Sainte-Adresse. Claude Monet. French, 1840–1926

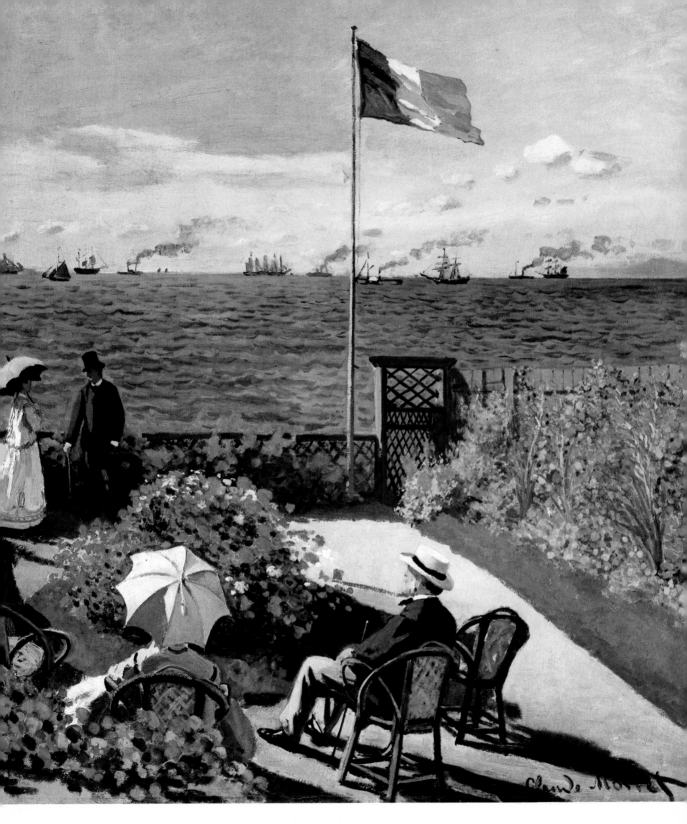

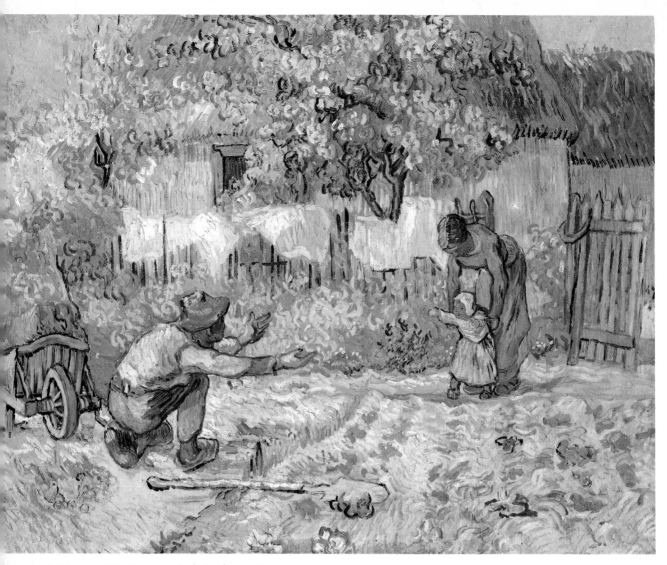

First Steps, c. 1890. Vincent van Gogh. Dutch, 1853–90

While putting in a hard day's work in the vegetable garden, a husband is delighted to be interrupted by his wife and child. Throwing his spade aside, he kneels to receive the little girl who is just learning to walk. This was one of the last – and happiest – paintings by Vincent van Gogh who, after fits of madness, died by his own hand here in the south of France in 1890.

Before the days of washing machines and dryers, the laundry got done as in the picture at right. Never was there a better way of finishing up than by hanging clothes and linens out to dry in the sun. Surely, too, there's never been a more charming study of a wash-day than this one, which Edouard Manet made towards the end of the last century in France.

Wash-day. Edouard Manet. French, 1832–83

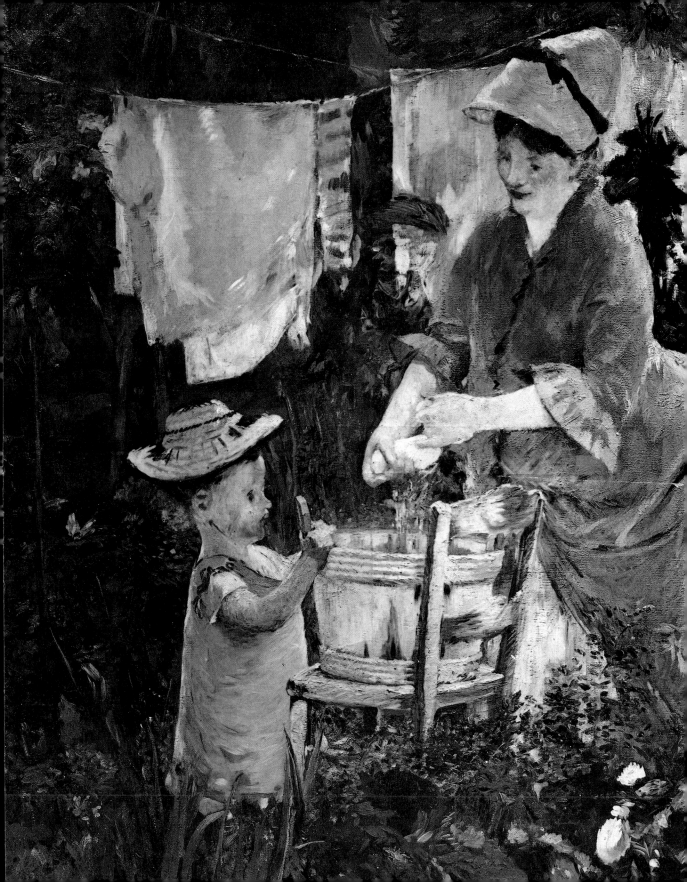

The six Flopsy Bunnies, below, enjoy a 'toes-up'
after stuffing themselves with lettuces in Mr
McGregor's garden. *The Tale of the Flopsy Bunnies*,
published in 1909, was one of the many books
written and illustrated by Beatrix Potter, in which
the garden played a very important role. Her first
story was about Peter Rabbit and his adventures,
also in Mr McGregor's garden. But Miss Potter was
sketching gardens, flowers and animals long before
then – she painted the cat sitting in a garden
during a visit to Wales in the spring of 1900.

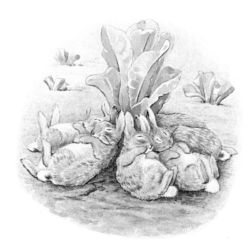

The Soporific Flopsy Bunnies.
From *The Tale of the Flopsy Bunnies,*
London, 1909. Beatrix Potter. English, 1866–1943

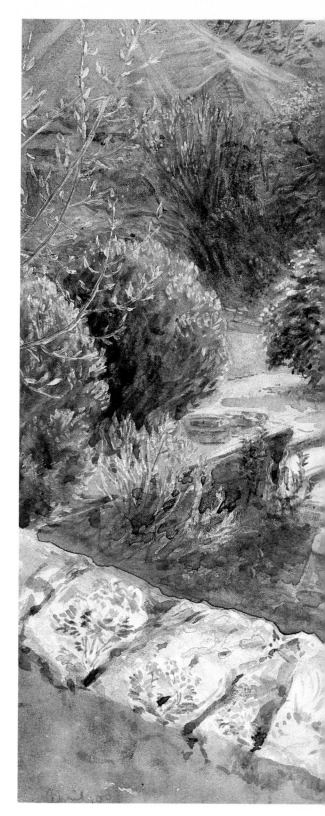

Garden at Tenby, Wales, 1900.
Beatrix Potter. English, 1866–1943

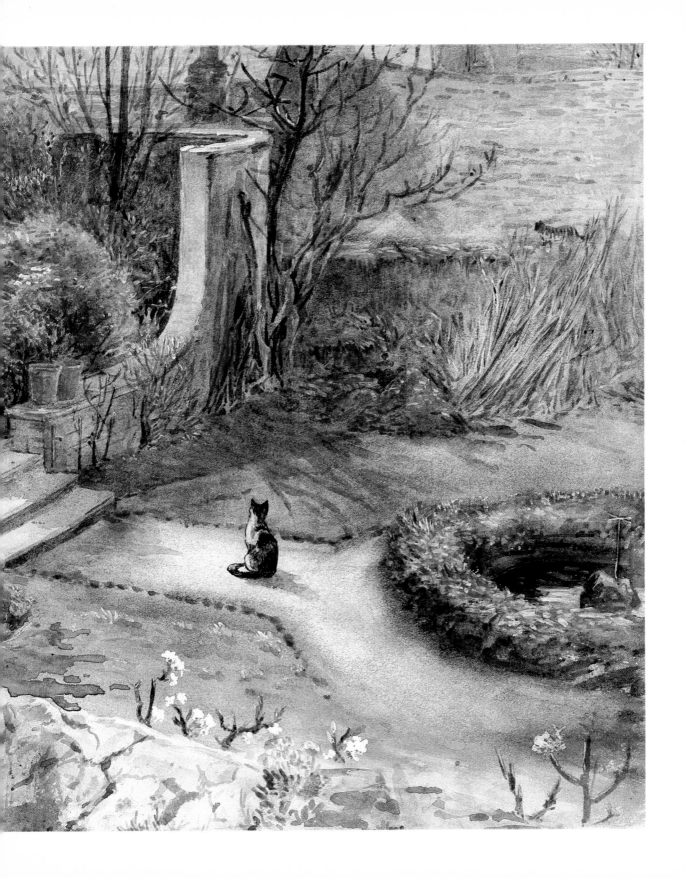

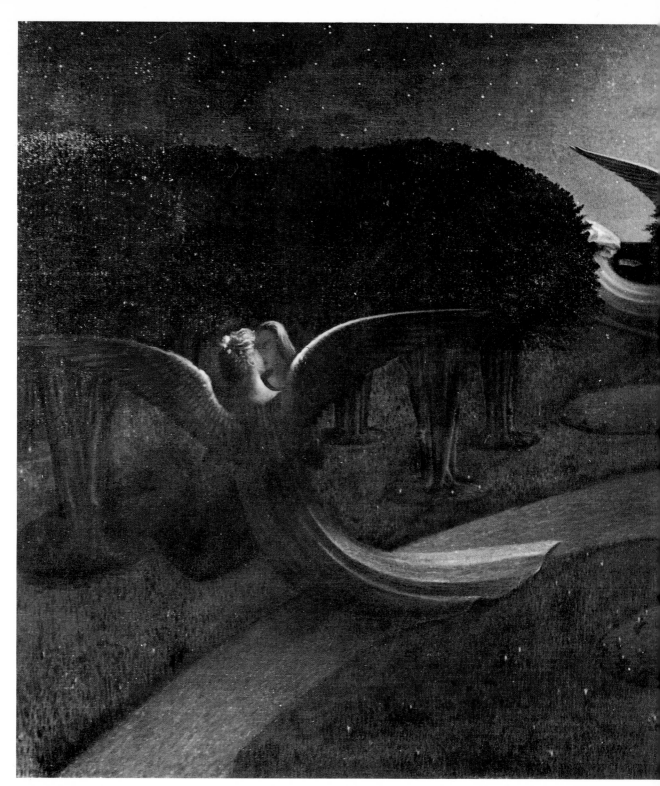

Angels in the Night, 1894. William Degourd de Nungues. Belgian, 19th c.

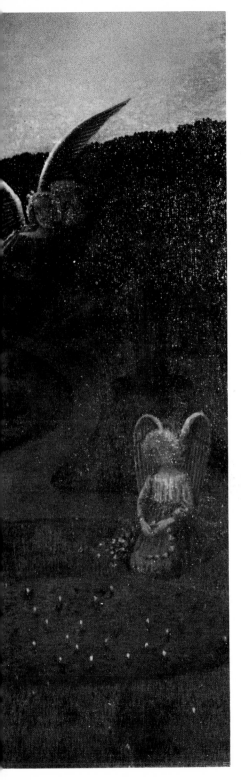

When an artist looks out across a beautiful garden on a still, starry night, anything poetic in the world – or from another world – is likely to stir his imagination. William Degourd de Nungues, in one of his 'flights to the beyond' saw angels gliding down a moonbeam and along the garden path in fond embrace.

Few artists in our own century have said more fantastic things in paintings than has the Surrealist, Salvador Dalí. Below, he envisions two dandelion ballerinas, looking rather like powder puffs in their tutus, dancing into the wind which, puff by puff, will blow their heads and tutus away.

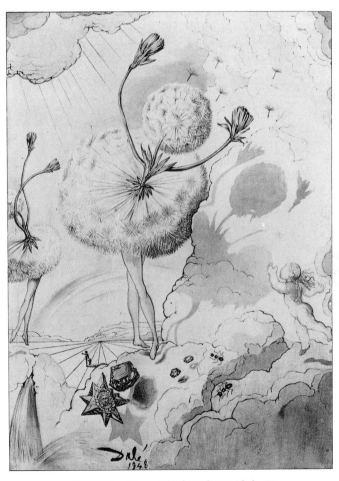

Dancing Dandelions. Salvador Dali. Spanish, b. 1904

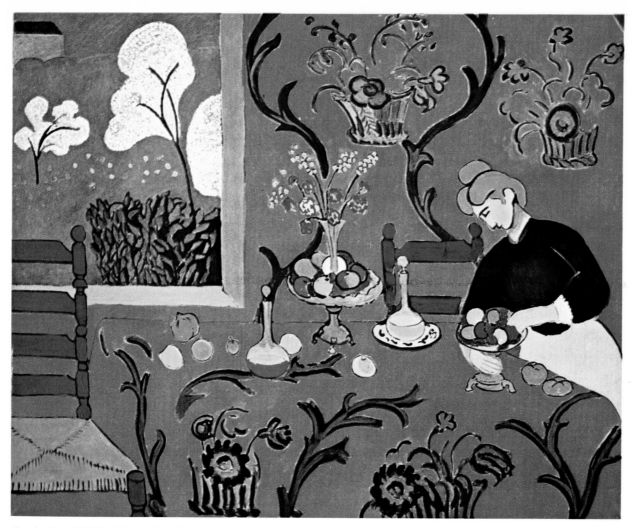

After the Meal, 1908. Henri Matisse. French, 1869–1954

Henri Matisse brought the outdoors indoors and covered the surface of the table and wall with a continuous pattern of flower, tree and fruit forms. Matisse spoke for the modern artist when he said that 'nobody can copy nature exactly . . . Instead, I must interpret nature and submit it to the spirit of the picture . . . the result must be a living harmony of tones, a harmony not unlike that of a musical composition.'

And so, between the earliest known pictures of gardens and Matisse's harmony in red – which, incidentally, he had first composed in blue and only later changed to red – we have covered some three thousand years, seen most styles of painting, and journeyed many thousands of miles looking at gardens that, to a large extent, have been born out of man's dreams of paradise.

ARTISTS AND ILLUSTRATIONS

REDOUTE, PIERRE-JOSEPH *A Rose Wreath*. 1.

RENOIR, PIERRE AUGUSTE *Girl with a Watering-can*. National Gallery of Art, Washington DC, Chester Dale Collection. 86.

REPTON, HUMPHREY Design for a pheasantry at the Royal Pavilion, Brighton. 58–59.

RIPANDA, JACOPO *Apollo and Daphne*. 13.

ROBERT, HUBERT *The Bathing Pool*. The Metropolitan Museum of Art, New York, Gift of J. Pierpont Morgan, 1917. 53.

SARGENT, JOHN SINGER *Carnation, Lily, Lily, Rose*. Tate Gallery, London. 84.

SAVERY, ROELANT *The Temptation in the Garden of Eden*. The Faringdon Collection Trust. 9.

SOSEN, MORI *Flowers of the Seasons*. Philadelphia Museum of Art, Given by Mrs John C. Atwood, Jr. 56.

TISSOT, JAMES *The Picnic*. Tate Gallery, London. 85.

TURNER, JOSEPH MALLORD WILLIAM *The Goddess of Discord Choosing the Apple of Contention in the Garden of the Hesperides*. Tate Gallery, London. 12.

VALCKENBORCH, LUCAS VAN *Spring Picnic with Elegant Company*. Kunsthistorisches Museum, Vienna. 33–34.

VERNET, HORACE *Lady Wearing an Italian Straw Hat and Chinese-style Wrap*. Victoria and Albert Museum, London. 68.

WALTHER, JOHANN *Blue Bird with Fruit*. Bibliothèque Nationale, Paris. 41.

WATTEAU, ANTOINE *Pleasures of the Dance*. By permission of the Governors of Dulwich Picture Gallery. 47.

WOOLLETT, WILLIAM *Swan at Kew Gardens*. 52.

YI OM *Puppy Playing with a Pheasant Feather*. Philadelphia Museum of Art, Purchased. 25.